"What a wonderful find Mark Daw *Shape of the River*, the teleplay in which Mark Twain's late years are sensitively portrayed. Horton understands Mark Twain. His artistry and southern roots lead him to the interior Mark Twain where the inner man watches in tortured silence the bravery of his family facing disasters. The pain is in the silences.

Mark Dawidziak's background research tracing the path this play followed from its germinating idea to the production, as well as his characterizations of all the participants from Fred Coe to Franchot Tone, makes for an entertaining story and an illuminating act of scholarship." —**Hal Holbrook**

"Horton Foote's poignant dramatization of the most painful years of Mark Twain's life, and Mark Dawidziak's fascinating essays on Mark Twain and television, make this book an intriguing contribution to television history and a welcome addition to the Mark Twain bookshelf." —**Shelley Fisher Fishkin**, author of *Lighting Out for the Territory: Reflections on Mark Twain and American Culture* and editor, *The Oxford Mark Twain*

"What a wonderful treasure: Here we have Horton Foote's remarkable play saved for posterity and Mark Dawidziak's thoughtful commentary to give it just the right framing. Here the real Twain—funny, larger-than-life, beset by tragedy, deeply thoughtful—comes alive. Riveting. I couldn't put it down." —**Ken Burns**, filmmaker

"It's hard to say which is more astounding here: Horton Foote's painstaking research and brilliant writing in his 1960 teleplay *The Shape of the River* about Samuel Clemens' late-in-life lecture tour and personal tragedies, or Mark Dawidziak's equally well-researched rediscovery and analysis of Foote's forgotten TV triumph. The play, the detective work, the interviews, the photos, the context—it's all so complete and compelling, even Mark Twain experts will learn from reading this book, and novices will become instant experts. For fans of classic TV, and especially for fans of Twain, this publication of the penultimate *Playhouse 90* script and the story behind it is the ultimate unexpected treat."

—**David Bianculli**, TV critic,
New York *Daily News* and
National Public Radio's *Fresh Air*

the shape of the River

HORTON FOOTE'S

the Shape of the River

The Lost Teleplay About Mark Twain

With History and Analysis by

Mark Dawidziak

To Rodi,
Many years,
Many tours,
Much love,

APPLAUSE
THEATRE & CINEMA BOOKS

Horton Foote's The Shape of the River: *The Lost Teleplay About Mark Twain With History and Analysis* by Mark Dawidziak

Cover photo courtesy of Library of Congress, Prints and Photographs Division: LC-USZ62-5513

Photographs from the *Playhouse 90* production of *The Shape of the River* are the copyright material of the CBS Photo Archive and are used with the permission of CBS. Other photographs are courtesy of the Elmira College Center for Mark Twain Studies, the Library of Congress, Jon Krampner, Hal Holbrook, and Horton Foote.

"Horton Foote's *The Shape of the River:* The Rediscovery of a Television Play About Mark Twain" was first presented as a paper at Elmira 2001: The Fourth International Conference on the State of Mark Twain Studies.

Art direction Michelle Thompson
Cover design Gabrielle F. Morgan
Book design Interrobang Design Studio

Library of Congress Cataloging-in-Publication Data
Foote, Horton. [Shape of the river]
Horton Foote's "The shape of the river" : the lost teleplay about Mark Twain, with history and analysis by Mark Dawidziak.
p. cm.
Includes bibliographical references and index.
ISBN 1-55783-519-5
1. Twain, Mark, 1835–1910—Drama.
2. Twain, Mark, 1835–1910—In literature.
3. Foote, Horton. Shape of the river.
4. Authors in literature.
5. Authors—Drama.
I. Dawidziak, Mark, 1956–
II. Title.
PS3511.O344 S53 2003
812'.54—dc21 2002153749

British Library Cataloging-in-Publication Data
A catalog record of this book is available from the British Library

APPLAUSE THEATRE & CINEMA BOOKS
151 West 46th Street, 8th Floor
New York, NY 10036

PHONE: (212) 575-9265
FAX: (646) 562-5852
EMAIL: info@applausepub.com
INTERNET: www.applausepub.com

SALES & DISTRIBUTION

NORTH AMERICA:
HAL LEONARD CORP.
7777 West Bluemound Road
P. O. Box 13819
Milwaukee, WI 53213

PHONE: (414) 774-3630
FAX: (414) 774-3259
EMAIL: halinfo@halleonard.com
INTERNET: www.halleonard.com

UK:
COMBINED BOOK SERVICES LTD.
Units I/K, Paddock Wood Distribution Centre
Paddock Wood, Tonbridge, Kent TN12 6UU

PHONE: (44) 01892 837171
FAX: (44) 01892 837272

United Kingdom

To the memory of Franchot Tone.

H.F.

To our friends at the Elmira College Center for Mark Twain Studies — the reports of their kindness have not been greatly exaggerated.

M.D.

Contents

Selected Quotes

"All say, 'How hard it is that we have to die'—a strange complaint to come from the mouths of people who have had to live."

—MARK TWAIN
Pudd'nhead Wilson (1894)

"Once and once again, and yet again and again, the black shadow that shall never be lifted where it falls, fell in his house..."

—WILLIAM DEAN HOWELLS
My Mark Twain (1910)

"In the circumstances, his ability to retain even a spark of humor and to write even unfinished fantasies was remarkable."

—HAMLIN HILL
Mark Twain: God's Fool (1973)

"Oh, this human life, this earthly life, this weary life!"

—MARK TWAIN
No. 44, The Mysterious Stranger

"I was struck by the overwhelming tragedy he had to face. I don't know how he stood it all as well as he did, really."

—HORTON FOOTE (2000)

Acknowledgments

Writing about the death of Henry H. Rogers in 1909, Mark Twain noted that the quality he most admired in the Standard Oil executive "was his unselfishness where a friend or a cause that was near his heart was concerned, and his native readiness to come forward and take vigorous hold of the difficulty involved and abolish it." Twain would be pleased to know that those who study his life and works also possess this same quality in limitless supply.

Indeed, if you venture into any area of Mark Twain research and shout for help, a battalion of experts will immediately respond to your call. If you ask for advice, it will arrive, in Twain's words, "by the cargo." If you feel lost and require guidance, dozens of reassuring hands will be at your back, gently pushing you in the right direction.

A call for assistance went out many times during the charting of *The Shape of the River.* Always ready to answer my call were two incredibly generous Twain scholars, Barbara Schmidt and Kevin Bochynski. They kept this project on course, and their suggestions were, to borrow a Twain simile, "as welcome as a corpse is to a coroner."

I also acknowledge my debt to an amazing team of "Twain friends": Gretchen Sharlow, the director of the Center for Mark Twain Studies at Elmira College; R. Kent Rasmussen, the author of two invaluable reference works, *Mark Twain A to Z* and *The Quotable Mark Twain*; Shelley Fisher Fishkin, whose insightful works on Twain include *Was Huck Black? Mark Twain and African-American Voices* and *Lighting Out for the Territory: Reflections on Mark Twain and American Culture;* and David Bianculli, the author of *Teleliteracy* and the television critic at the *New York Daily News*. I am deeply grateful for their expert advice and their warm encouragement.

The rediscovery of Horton Foote's *Playhouse 90* drama first took shape as a paper presented in August 2001 at Elmira College's Fourth International Conference on the State of Mark Twain Studies. It is unlikely I would have taken this academic step without the backing and bolstering of those Twainiacs already cited; as well as Robert H. Hirst, general editor of the Mark Twain Papers at the University of California in Berkeley; Thomas A. Tenney, editor of the *Mark Twain Journal*; Hal Holbrook, who makes Twain come alive on stage and in discussion; and Robert Slotta, the Twain collector who never stops digging or sharing.

For graciously summoning recollections and memories from four decades ago, I give my sincere thanks to Shirley Knight, the late John Frankenheimer, and Sandy Kenyon. I am indebted to David Lombard for his help in locating pictures from the CBS Photo Archive. For copies of the network's original press releases, I must acknowledge the prompt response of veteran CBS publicist Michael Silver. For photographs of television pioneer Fred Coe, deepest appreciation to biographer Jon Krampner. And I express my gratitude to Mark Woodhouse at Elmira College for assembling a remarkable package of photographs and newspaper clippings.

I'd also like to recognize the belief and support demonstrated by John Cerullo and Mark Glubke at Applause Theatre & Cinema Books. And, of course, there's no way to adequately express my thanks to Horton Foote—first, for writing this intriguing play about Mark Twain, then, about forty years later, for putting up with my persistent questions about it. File this in the category labeled understatement: It is an unbelievable honor to be along for the ride with the likes of Mark Twain and Horton Foote.

There's also no adequate way to acknowledge the patience, understanding, and love demonstrated throughout this process by the "home team," Sara and Becky. To again borrow a Twain sentiment: wheresoever they are, there is Eden.

—MARK DAWIDZIAK

Horton Foote's The Shape of the River:

The Rediscovery of a Television Play About Mark Twain

BY MARK DAWIDZIAK

Mark Twain decreed that there had never been such a thing as an uninteresting life. Inside each person, he explained, "there is a drama, a comedy, and a tragedy."[1]

But four decades ago, most Americans did not associate the word "tragedy" with the author whose beloved children's classics include *The Adventures of Tom Sawyer* (1876) and *The Prince and the Pauper* (1881). Indeed, the general impression of Mark Twain in 1960 was still pretty sunny. He was the iconic writer who had given the world such cherished characters as mischievous Tom and his good-hearted friend, Huck Finn. He was the genial folk humorist—Missouri's geographic and philosophical link between Philadelphia's Benjamin Franklin in the eighteenth century and Oklahoma's Will Rogers in the twentieth. He was the grandfatherly man of letters dressed in a white suit, dispensing sly witticisms between puffs on his ever-present cigar.

This was the image crafted by Albert Bigelow Paine in his three-volume authorized biography published in 1912. It was the sentimental image fiercely protected by the writer's only surviving child, Clara.[2] It was also the image promoted by Hollywood in such films as *The Adventures of Mark Twain,* an entertaining but highly sanitized 1944 Warner Bros. biography starring Fredric March. While this movie more than suggested that there were great turns of comedy and drama in Twain's life, it made no concession to tragedy. This was a dimension of the writer largely shielded from the public.

Yet there is an almost Lear-like tragedy to be found in the life of the man born Samuel Langhorne Clemens in 1835, and it is this tragedy that another Southern writer, Horton Foote, gave powerful shape to in an ambitious television drama titled *The Shape of the River*. Covering the last fifteen years of the writer's life, this ninety-minute production was aired May 2, 1960, on the acclaimed CBS series *Playhouse 90*.

Over the next forty years, the popular image of Mark Twain would take on increasingly darker hues. Through such landmark biographies as Justin Kaplan's *Mr. Clemens and Mark Twain* in 1966 and Hamlin Hill's *Mark Twain: God's Fool* in 1973, Americans began to learn just how much pain and paradox were wrapped around the final, tortured phase of Twain's life. Remarkably, without the benefit of the revelations in those books, Foote presented a Mark Twain relentlessly stalked by sadness and what CBS publicity material described as "profound personal tragedy."[3]

Casting more than a few psychologically dark shadows on the sunny Twain image, Kaplan's biography won both the National Book Award and the Pulitzer Prize. Concentrating on the last ten years of Twain's life, Hill's book dissected the "authorized" version, establishing the importance of secretary Isabel Lyon, a member of the Clemens inner circle expunged from the official record by Clara and Paine. Lyon was exiled from the Clemens household when she wound up on the losing end of a 1909 power struggle that pitted her against Clara and Paine. Although there are no references to Lyon in Foote's drama, *The Shape of the River* dwells so unremittingly on the darkness of those last fifteen years, it in many ways foreshadows the changes in our perception of Mark Twain.

"Mark Twain was immensely interested in his destination after death," Hill wrote in *God's Fool*. "The truth is inescapable that, wherever he went after he died, much of the last decade of his life, he lived in hell."[4] This is precisely the terrible feeling one gets when viewing *The Shape of the River*. What Hill proved so convincingly with the scholar's tools in 1973, Foote demonstrated with a dramatist's sense in 1960. To be sure, his play offered no facts unknown to serious Twain scholars fifty years after the author's death in 1910. Yet it did distill the established record of tragedy in a manner that was as forceful and convincing as it was touching. Foote dug deep into the published works on Twain, extracting eloquent moments that revealed the complex man behind the popular image.

But was America ready to accept a "dark" Twain in 1960? It doesn't seem so. The program received poor ratings against reruns of ABC's *Cheyenne* and NBC's struggling *Riverboat* (which, ironically, starred Burt Reynolds as the pilot of a Mississippi steamboat). A veteran of television's golden age of live drama, the soft-spoken Foote does not go so far as to claim that the production was ahead of its time—or ahead of the biographers. Foote does believe, however, that viewers were reluctant in 1960 to stick with a Twain beset by one horrifying tragedy after another. "They didn't want to hear it," he said. "They still wanted to think of him as a humorist and a family author."[5]

Nonetheless, Foote remains fond and proud of *The Shape of the River*. He would go on to win two screenwriting Oscars (for his adaptation of Harper Lee's *To Kill a Mockingbird* and his original screenplay *Tender Mercies*), an Emmy (for his adaptation of William Faulkner's *Old Man*), and a Pulitzer Prize (for *The Young Man from Atlanta*), but memories of *The Shape of the River* remain vivid more than forty years after it was telecast.

"I don't even know if a copy exists," he told me during a 1997 interview. "Isn't that awful? Franchot Tone played Twain, and he was quite remarkable. At the time, I remember being tremendously moved by Tone's performance. My archives would love to have a copy. Not even the Museum of Broadcasting has a copy. We've checked."[6]

It might have ended there, marked down as a curious footnote to the writer's career, had it not been for a chance encounter in cyberspace. A few months later, tireless Twain researcher Barbara Schmidt posted a question about *The Shape of the River* on the Mark Twain Forum, the Internet gathering place for members of the Mark Twain Circle and assorted Twainiacs. I shared Foote's comments with her, and, in a matter of weeks, she had located a video copy of the *Playhouse 90* drama in the CBS vaults. The network agreed to release a copy of the program to Foote, who agreed to make a copy for me (Foote's pool man, equipped with the knowledge of how to hook up two VCRs, did the actual dubbing).

Foote also agreed to a follow-up interview, recalling what he could about how the production was researched, cast, and prepared. He began with his affection for Mark Twain.

"My true influences as a vastly obsessive young reader were Mark Twain and Willa Cather," said Foote, who was born in 1916 and grew up in the Gulf-coast Texas town of Wharton. "I instinctively knew that Mark Twain was a great writer. When I was growing up, it seemed that every Southern house had a collected edition of Mark Twain. I can still see them sitting on the shelf. And I practically lived inside of *Tom Sawyer* and *Huck Finn*. As a young boy, I wanted to be Tom—not Huck. I loved Huck, but I really didn't want to be Huck. I didn't think I could make that."[7]

Later, as a young writer, Foote still counted Twain among his primary literary idols: "I was very fond of *Life on the Mississippi*. You feel the authenticity of his works, and that had a profound influence on me. He had a total sense of place. So I never approached him as a historical figure. Twain was a very real presence to me."[8]

So Foote was delighted when legendary television producer Fred Coe eagerly agreed in the mid-fifties to his idea for a drama about the last fifteen years of Mark Twain's life. At the helm of the *Philco TV Playhouse* (started in 1948) and the equally celebrated *Goodyear TV Playhouse* (started in 1951), Coe had recruited such promising young writers—and future Oscar winners—as Foote and Paddy Chayefsky (whose 1953 *Goodyear* drama, *Marty*, became the first live show to "propel a television writer to national prominence"[9]).

It was the peak of television's golden age of live drama, and nobody was more responsible for putting the luster on that marvelous era than Fred Coe. His earliest network experience was in 1945 as the thirty-year-old production manager at NBC. He then worked briefly for innovative producer Worthington Miner on the CBS anthology series *Studio One*. But Coe's reign as the infant medium's leading impresario truly began on October 3, 1948, with the premiere of NBC's *Philco TV Playhouse*. From 1951 to 1955, *Philco* alternated with *Goodyear TV Playhouse* in the 9–10 p.m. Sunday time slot.

With the film studios viewing the networks as the enemy, big-name actors were in short supply for the live dramatic anthologies that soon would bring some badly needed prestige to this unformed thing called television. Studio bosses threatened to tear up the contracts of any Hollywood stars defecting to the upstart rival medium. Coe, working with NBC's programming chief, Pat Weaver, decided to make his own stars: young writers crafting works specifically designed for the new medium. *Philco* began with adaptations of Broadway plays and novels, musical productions, and even some biographies, but it was the original drama that put the golden-age anthologies on the map.

In addition to Chayefsky and Foote, the writers working for *Philco* and *Goodyear* included Gore Vidal, J.P. Miller, Reginald Rose, Ernest Kinoy, Robert Alan Arthur, and Tad Mosel. About the only "young lion" not penning scripts for Coe during this era was Rod Serling, whose work was appearing on such golden-age anthologies as Miner's *Studio One*, *The U.S. Steel Hour*, *Hallmark Hall of Fame*, and *Kraft Television Theatre*.

Coe's "the play's the thing" strategy paid dividends, and his *Philco/Goodyear* tandem also started establishing an impressive roster of directors (including Delbert Mann and Arthur Penn) and actors (Paul Newman, Rod Steiger, and Charlton Heston among them). His "ability to nurture writers and team them with the right directors was truly impressive,"[10] noted *New York Daily News* television critic and Mark Twain Circle member David Bianculli.

A writer with several plays to his credit by the late forties, Foote had started an independent repertory company with director Vincent J. Donehue in Washington, D.C. Coe, who had been Donehue's roommate in college, suggested that the duo go to work for NBC.

Foote's earliest television work was not for Coe, but the collaboration got off to an auspicious start in March 1953. That's when NBC aired *The Trip to Bountiful*, Foote's story of elderly Carrie Watts, a widow who "runs away," determined to visit the Texas town where she was born. Lillian Gish played Carrie, a role she reprised for the three-act stage version that ran on Broadway for thirty-nine performances in late 1953. Geraldine Page won an Academy Award for her portrayal of Carrie in Foote's 1985 film version. She was the third star voted an Oscar in a movie written by Foote, following Gregory Peck as Atticus Finch in *To Kill a Mockingbird* (1962) and Robert Duvall as a down-and-out country singer piecing his life back together in *Tender Mercies* (1983).

By the end of 1954, Foote had written nine more plays for Coe, including *The Midnight Caller*, *Expectant Relations*, and *A Young Lady of Property*, which featured Joanne Woodward and Kim Stanley, an actress Foote's wife, Lillian, had "discovered." She had appeared in the brief 1952 Broadway run of Foote's *The Chase* (a play he later turned into a novel), but Stanley became a star playing the title role in the 1954 Broadway production of another Foote drama, *The Traveling Lady*.

Again emphasizing his spotlight-the-writers philosophy, Coe launched a new NBC anthology series, *Playwrights '56*, in October 1955. The short-lived program alternated with *Armstrong Circle Theatre* in the

9:30–10:30 p.m. Tuesday time slot. Foote's original plays for this program included *Flight*, which aired February 28, 1956. The drama starred Stanley as woman in flight from a failing marriage. It was during this time that Foote began talking to Coe about a production exploring Mark Twain's last years.

"I remember the genesis of this project quite well," Foote explained. "It wasn't originally supposed to be for *Playhouse 90*. Fred Coe commissioned me to write this for another program he had at the time, *Playwrights '56*. He asked me for something, and I asked him to let me try something on Mark Twain. You see, I always wanted to adapt *Huckleberry Finn*. But people only wanted to do it as a caricature. I still want to do it, if I can get anybody to do it correctly—not those cheap Hollywood versions. No one thought that was feasible, so I said, 'Well, I'm interested in Mark Twain, so let me see what else I can come up with.' And I went to work."[11]

The producer was impressed with Foote's concept, but *Playwrights '56* was canceled by NBC. Coe then moved to CBS and joined producers Martin Manulis and Herbert Brodkin on the team behind *Playhouse 90*, which has been accurately described as "the pinnacle of live drama from TV's 'Golden Age.'"[12] During its storied run from October 1956 to May 1960, the anthology aired ten dramas by Rod Serling (including *Requiem for a Heavyweight, The Comedian, A Town Has Turned to Dust,* and *The Velvet Alley*), as well as works by writers Coe knew from the *Philco/Goodyear* days: Rose, Miller, and Foote.

Unlike its illustrious predecessors in the dramatic anthology field, *Playhouse 90*, as the title suggests, occupied ninety minutes of prime-time real estate. Expanding from the traditional hour, the series allowed television's finest writers the chance to more fully develop themes and characters.

Some of the most notable golden-age dramas were produced for *Playhouse 90*: Miller's *The Days of Wine and Roses*, William Gibson's *The Miracle Worker*, and, of course, Serling's *Requiem for a*

Heavyweight. Among Foote's works for *Playhouse 90* were two adaptations of Faulkner stories, *Old Man* and *Tomorrow*. Late in the series' prime-time life, Coe called Foote: "Remember the play you wrote about Mark Twain? I want to do it for *Playhouse 90*."[13]

By 1960, *Playhouse 90* was no longer a weekly series. Alternating between live productions and videotape, episodes were being aired as occasional specials. Although Foote remembers *The Shape of the River* as a live production, it was videotaped in Hollywood at Television City, the CBS studio facility that opened in 1952. It should be pointed out, however, that this process often was described as "live on tape." This was because the videotape machines of the day were primitive and shooting with them was expensive. As such, the cameras rarely stopped and minor goofs were allowed to air. When, for instance, an actor stumbled over a line, as Tone did in a couple of longer monologues, nobody yelled, "Cut!" A slight miscue was left in. Today, the scene would be quickly and cheaply reshot.

Viewers tuned to CBS at 8 p.m. on May 2, 1960 were told that *The Texan*, *Father Knows Best*, and *The Danny Thomas Show* would not be seen that night. They were being preempted for a special presentation of *Playhouse 90*, "brought to you by Camel, America's real cigarette that gives you real smoking satisfaction each and every time you light up," the All-State Insurance Companies, and "your gas company." During an early commercial, actor James Daly—father of *Cagney & Lacey* star Tyne Daly and *Wings* regular Tim Daly—asked the immortal question, "Are you smoking more now and enjoying it less?" Given the number of cheroots Sam Clemens puffed his way through in a day, it would have been interesting to hear his reply to the pithy Camel pitch.

Within the month, intriguingly enough, Daly would be playing Twain in an NBC adaptation of *Roughing It* (the writer's 1872 book about his years in the Nevada Territory and California).

The Shape of the River begins in the late spring of 1895 at the Clemens' enchanting home in Hartford. The production opens with a picture of this fabulous house, where Mark Twain and his family lived from 1874 to the early 1890s. A gaudy nineteen-room structure, dazzling and eccentric in design, Number 351 Farmington Avenue was described by biographer Justin Kaplan as "part steamboat, part medieval stronghold, and part cuckoo clock."[14]

Hamlin Hill called the ornate dwelling Twain's "deliberate revenge for the poverty of his own childhood."[15] And Twain himself said "our house was not unsentient matter—it had heart and a soul and eyes to see us with... We never came home from an absence that its face did not light up and speak out its eloquent welcome—and we could not enter it unmoved."[16]

By 1895, the Clemens family could no longer afford to maintain the treasured Hartford house, which Foote knew from his extensive research. Twain and his wife had closed it four years earlier and had moved temporarily to Europe to cut down on expenses. But the playwright's instincts led him to Hartford for his opening sequences. He chose to start *The Shape of the River* on Farmington Avenue in order to give his work the proper dramatic and spiritual point of origin. Home is where the heart is, the maxim assures us, and their hearts surely were in the Hartford home.

It was a warm household where Sam and Livy Clemens entertained a wide circle of friends and raised their three daughters: Susy, Clara, and Jean. However, little writing actually was done in Hartford, thanks to social engagements, business obligations, and ever-present distractions. Instead, most of Twain's writing was done during the summers the family spent in Elmira, New York, at Quarry Farm, the home of Livy's sister, Susan Langdon Crane. Twain spent his days in a snug and isolated octagonal study Aunt Sue had built for him on the grounds in 1874.

It was a period of great happiness and productivity for the author known to the world as Mark Twain. During this time he wrote *The Adventures of Tom Sawyer* (1876), *A Tramp Abroad* (1880), *The Prince and the Pauper* (1881), *Life on the Mississippi* (1883), *Huckleberry Finn* (1884), and *A Connecticut Yankee in King Arthur's Court* (1889).

But as *The Shape of the River* explains, Twain's fortunes had faded due to disastrous investments, bad business decisions, poor economic conditions, and mismanagement by others. The extent of the collapse was spelled out in 1894 when his failing publishing firm, Charles L. Webster & Company, entered into voluntary bankruptcy. Almost sixty and about $100,000 in debt, the ruined writer was determined to crawl his way back to solvency in a manner that would appease both an army of creditors and his own fiery conscience.

With his wife and three daughters living in reduced circumstances, he heroically resolved to repay all his debts, dollar for dollar. The ninety-six creditors would have settled for less—much less, probably fifty cents on the dollar. Yet Twain would not settle for anything less than complete repayment. He stuck by this resolve, even though Standard Oil Company director Henry Huttleston Rogers, an admirer who in 1893 quickly became a close a friend, told him that ninety-eight percent of men who failed in business "never get up again." Merely getting up would not satisfy Twain. He would honor the debts to the last cent, earning the right to hold his head high and to again "live in literature."[17]

"In the thick of the fight there is cheer," he wrote to Livy. "You only seem to see rout, retreat and dishonored colors dragging in the dirt—whereas none of these things exist. There is temporary defeat, but no dishonor—and we will march again."[18]

The only path open to him was one he had come to loathe—the lecture platform, where he had reigned as America's foremost humorous speaker. With Rogers' help, Twain devised a plan that would remove the shadow of bankruptcy. He would lecture around the world and then write a travel book about his trip. Beginning in Cleveland on July 15, 1895, he would make about 140 appearances on five continents.

Susy, Twain's oldest child, and Jean, the youngest, stayed in America with the family's devoted servant, Katy Leary. Accompanying Twain on his marathon journey were Livy and their middle child, Clara.

"Do you remember, Livy," Twain later asked his wife, "the hellish struggle it was to settle on making that lecture trip around the world? How we fought the idea, the horrible idea, the heart-torturing idea. I almost an old man, with ill health, carbuncles [painful inflammation of the skin and underlying tissue], bronchitis and rheumatism. I, with patience worn to rags, I was to pack my bag and be jolted around the devil's universe for what? To pay debts that were not even of my making... But once the idea of that infernal trip struck us we couldn't shake it."[19]

It is here, with the infernal idea having struck, that Foote begins *The Shape of the River*, structured as a three-act drama for the ninety-minute time period. Sam Clemens is about to embark on his round-the-world lecture tour. He is talking to Henry Rogers—played by veteran stage actor Larry Gates—about the collapse of his fortunes. Although this captain of capitalism would have been largely unknown to even a *Playhouse 90* audience of 1960, Rogers proves a dramatically useful figure in this opening scene. First, he was more than Twain's financial advisor at this crucial moment of his life. Rogers was Twain's financial savior, and, as such, he's the ideal expert to quickly provide some necessary background on the Clemens family's troubles. Yet Foote also knows that Rogers' solid business sense and industrial-strength grasp of money matters will supply an immediate and intriguing contrast to Twain's shaky approach to speculation. Small wonder that their friendship has fascinated a battalion of biographers.

Foote could only hint at why this was such an unlikely friendship. Twain, after all, had done his share of thundering at Wall Street barons. Now, at this moment of crisis, a Standard Oil boss was offering a way out of the darkness. The irony was not lost on Twain, who had indicted the excesses of the post-Civil War era, dubbing it the Gilded Age. The writer who had used his pen to slash at the buccaneers of business fully realized that "the only man who is lavishing his sweat and blood to save me and mine from starvation, is a Standard Oil fiend."[20]

Commenting on the friendship, Twain admitted that there was no question about Rogers being a pirate. But the robber baron nicknamed "Hell

Hound" Rogers by his enemies, cheerfully owned up to being a pirate, and Twain liked him for it. While probably true, this assessment only scratches the surface of the relationship. It's also probable that Twain saw a good deal of irony in his own mixed feelings about high finance.

Rogers, after all, epitomized everything Mark Twain admired and despised. All his life, Justin Kaplan observed, Twain "dreamed of being rich," yet "at the same time believed that money was evil and fostered evil... As a businessman and provincial plutocrat, he embraced business values, but as writer, critic, and moralist, he rejected them and cast a savage eye upon American society."[21]

Fueling this savagery was Twain's keen awareness of his shortcomings as a businessman. With all his contempt for America's "money fever," he never could resist the get-rich-quick scheme or the glittering speculation that promised vast profits. Quoting a passage from Mark Twain's *Autobiography* almost word-for-word, Foote has the writer tell Rogers that "all through my life I have been the easy prey of the cheap adventurer. He came, he lied, he robbed and went his way and the next one arrived by the next train and scraped up what was left. Instead of sticking to what I know, I have to try every fool scheme that comes along, that gives promises of sudden riches."

Mark Twain, the humorist and moralist, was able to take dead aim at the foibles of Sam Clemens, the businessman and Gilded-Age speculator: "Instead of sticking to what I know...," and what he knew was writing. What he didn't know was how to stick to just writing.

Many Twain biographers have made a habit of speculating about and digging for psychological riches in that area known as duality. Understandably tantalized by such immense contradictions, they've worked the claim mighty hard, tunneling deep into the writer's psyche and his writings for evidence of a dual nature—unquestionably with just cause.

First, as already mentioned, there are those deeply divided attitudes toward the pursuit of wealth. Then, there are the bitter denunciations of "the damned human race" that seem no less heartfelt than his need for the public's adoration and affection. There are also the twins or look-alikes in such novels as *The Prince and the Pauper* and *Pudd'nhead Wilson.* Additionally, there are the characters who, in a Jekyll-and-Hyde manner, seem to illuminate two contradictory sides of his personality. For instance, Tom Sawyer and Huck Finn are said to represent the two aspects of his dual nature (Tom, the exhibitionist craving fame and fortune; Huck, the good-hearted soul, seeking peace and content with simple pleasures). Was Mark Twain the character Sam Clemens created and used as a comic mouthpiece? Or, is it possible that Mark Twain was the public buffoon Sam Clemens tired of and wished he could send into permanent exile? Alternatively, did Sam Clemens grow into Mark Twain, America's towering literary figure of the nineteenth century? The swamp of duality is a tricky one. Was the Huck side of his nature best represented by Sam or Mark? In fact, was he Sam or was he Mark?

It's a topic that can keep two Twain scholars debating for hours. But there's good evidence that Twain himself never settled this question in his mind. For one thing, what's in a name? Interestingly enough, he was known by different names to different people. To Livy (played by Katharine Bard in *The Shape of the River*), he was Youth, the nickname she always used for him. To his brother Orion and old Missouri friends, he was Sam. To author and critic William Dean Howells, a close friend for about forty years, he was Clemens (in the Victorian-Era tradition of even intimate acquaintances referring to each other by last names; and there was no lack of warmth in Twain's referring to two of his most sympathetic confidants as Howells and Rogers). But to Congregationalist pastor Joseph Twichell, a friend certainly as dear to him as Howells and Rogers, he was always Mark. In this version of the name game, Twichell was Joe. Twain even signed his letters to Twichell and others as Mark.

You can read four different esteemed books about Mark Twain and find biographers referring to him in four different ways. In his *Mark Twain's America* (1932), Bernard DeVoto called him Mark. In *Mr. Clemens and Mark Twain*, Kaplan opted for Clemens. In her two books on the writer, Shelley Fisher Fishkin referred to him as Twain. And in his 1997 biography, Andrew Hoffman went with Sam. So what's a *Playhouse 90* writer to do? Youth? Sam? Clemens? Mark? Twain?

Leaving the duality debate to later biographers, Foote has Livy call him Youth, the daughters call him Papa, and almost everyone else call him Sam. It was an understandable and wholly acceptable simplification of the rather murky moniker issue.

The first act of *The Shape of the River* continues with the Clemens family's last-minute packing for the lecture tour. Assisting Livy is Katy Leary (Katherine Squire) and Jean (Jane McArthur). Clara (Nancy Rennick) returns home from shopping while Susy (Shirley Knight), an aspiring singer, is at the piano working on vocal exercises.

The scene progresses with Sam discovering a book Susy started writing in 1885. It's her biography of him, and the words Foote has Twain read to Livy are taken directly from portions printed in his *Autobiography*: "We are a very happy family. We consist of Papa, Mama, Jean, Clara and me. It is Papa I am writing about, and I shall have no trouble in not knowing what to say about him, as he is a *very* striking character."[22]

The scene shifts to the Hartford railroad station, where Susy, Jean, and Katy bid a tearful farewell to Sam, Livy, and Clara. They actually left for Cleveland from Elmira, where Twain had spent almost two months preparing his lectures. Traveling with them for the North American leg of the tour was lecture manager James Burton Pond and his wife, Martha. Hard choices had to be made in order to cover fifteen years of Twain's life in ninety minutes, so Foote sacrificed the Ponds, Elmira, and dear old Joe Twichell. Only those with something more than a casual interest in Mark Twain would realize they were missing.

From Cleveland, the tour proceeded to Michigan, Minnesota, Montana, and Washington. The route then took them from Vancouver to Hawaii to Australia to India to South Africa to Great Britain. They landed in England on July 31, 1896, happy in the knowledge that Susy, Jean, and Katy soon would be sailing from New York to join them.

Waiting for them in Southampton was a cable that explained Susy was ill and departure had been delayed. A subsequent cable assured them that recovery was certain but would be longer than expected. A worried Livy and Clara sailed for America to care for Susy, who was generally assumed to be Twain's favorite daughter. He was alone, in the dining room of a rented house in Guilford, when a cable was slipped into his hand on August 18: "Susy was peacefully released today."

"It is one of the mysteries of our nature," Twain observed in his *Autobiography*, "that a man, all unprepared, can receive a thunder-stroke like that and live."[23]

Here was what should have been a moment of monumental triumph for Mark Twain. The year of penance was done. The family was to be reunited. But at the very conclusion of the grand tour, the thunder-stroke fell, bringing devastation and anguish. If Foote had written such a shattering turn of events into another play, critics might have justifiably accused him of wallowing in melodrama. Twain would have known how to answer those critics. In *Following the Equator*, the book published a year after Susy's death, Twain concluded that, "Truth is stranger than fiction, but it is because Fiction is obliged to stick to possibilities; Truth isn't." Twain's life bears this out, filled as it was with amazing coincidences, stunning losses, fabulous comebacks, and heart-rending tragedy.

Susy died of spinal meningitis in the Hartford house, where she, Jean, and Katy had stopped before the planned trip to England. Also with her were Aunt Sue Crane and Joe Twichell. Foote reduces the number of people present to one, Katy, yet Shirley Knight's actions and dialogue in this scene are almost all in keeping with the record left by witnesses: Susy's raging fever did cause delirium, she did in fact go blind near the end, and she did indeed caress Katy's face and say, "Mama."

Susy was laid to rest in Elmira's Woodlawn Cemetery, near her brother, Langdon, who had died in 1872 at just nineteen months. Foote accurately quotes the epitaph Sam and Livy chose to be engraved on their daughter's headstone. They were lines adapted from a poem by Australian writer Robert Richardson:

Warm summer sun, shine brightly here,
Warm Southern wind, blow softly here,
Green sod above, lie light, lie light,
Good night, dear heart, good night, good night.

Twain was no stranger to tragedy before the crippling financial setbacks and the death of Susy. An older brother, Benjamin, had died when Twain was only six years old. A younger brother, Henry, was killed when the steamboat Pennsylvania blew up in 1858. There was also the death of his infant son, Langdon, in 1872, and both Twain's mother and mother-in-law died in 1890.

Yet a seismic shift had occurred during this period covered by the first act of Foote's *Playhouse 90* script. Twain himself recognized it in a letter to Rogers. Before the time depicted in *The Shape of the River*, he seemed to live a charmed life: "All my life I have stumbled upon lucky chances of large size... I couldn't shake off the confidence of a life-time in luck."[24] The luck ran out as the debts mounted. Then the tragedies mounted as the debts were paid off.

Underscoring the heartbreak of these years, each act of *The Shape of the River* ends with a death. The first act ends, as previously hinted at, with Susy's death in 1896. The second act opens with Twain's 1902 visit to his Missouri boyhood home in Hannibal and ends with the June 1904 death of his wife, Livy, in Florence, Italy. The third act begins with Twain's seventieth birthday dinner at Delmonico's and concludes with the death of Jean on December 24, 1909, at her father's last home, Stormfield. An epileptic, she died of an apparent heart attack triggered by a seizure during a cold morning bath.

"Well," he told Paine after Jean's death, "I suppose you have heard of this final disaster." He had survived his wife, three of his four children, and all of his siblings.

The record of losses since 1895 was staggering. His oldest brother,

Orion, died in 1897. Charles Dudley Warner, his collaborator on *The Gilded Age* (1873), died in 1900. His sister, Pamela, died in 1904. Secretary of State John Hay, an author and good friend, died in 1905. Jim Gillis, a prospecting buddy from his California days, died in 1907. And two close friends, Rogers and author-editor Richard Watson Gilder, died in 1909. These were deaths not even mentioned in *The Shape of the River.*

Foote's script ends in late December 1909. Twain, seventy-four when Jean died, had less than four months to live. He was survived by Clara and her husband, pianist Ossip Grabilowitsch, Susan Crane, Katy Leary, Howells, Twichell, Paine, and Livy's brother, Charles Langdon.

"The research was intense," Foote recalled. "I got everything I could possibly get hold of on Mark Twain. I was struck by the overwhelming tragedy he had to face. I don't know how he stood it all as well as he did, really. And I decided to focus on the last years. Nobody suggested that. That was completely my idea, and I wish I could say I was conscious of being ahead of the time. I just remember being struck by the poignancy of those last years."[25]

When putting together the original script for *Playwrights '56*, Foote used Paine's three-volume *Mark Twain: A Biography* (1912), the two-volume 1917 edition of *Mark Twain's Letters*, the two-volume *Mark Twain's Autobiography* (edited by Paine and published in 1924), Mary Lawton's rendering of Katy Leary's memories in *A Lifetime with Mark Twain* (1925), Clara Clemens' *My Father: Mark Twain* (1931), DeVoto's *Mark Twain's America*, DeLancey Ferguson's *Mark Twain: Man and Legend* (1943), and *The Love Letters of Mark Twain* (edited by Dixon Wecter and published in 1949).

For a rewrite completed about four years later, Foote probably consulted Charles Neider's just-published version of *The Autobiography of Mark Twain* (1959). He also used the 1935 collection, *Mark Twain's Notebook*, for such details as Susy's feverish ranting about the trolley cars going up and down "for Mark Twain's daughter."[26] Some fudging of facts was necessary, of course, but his research was impressive—even by today's standards. Much of the dialogue is authentic Twain, and such friends as Howells, Rogers, and Paine are portrayed reasonably true to life (even if Leif Erickson was far too tall and lean for the shorter, rounder Howells).

Foote also used a generous sampling of Twain wit and wisecracks to lighten the otherwise somber mood. The mounting losses would have been unendurable to the viewer if not for humor. Again, Foote is following Twain's advice: "Humor is the great thing, the saving thing, after all."[27]

Although the duality question is left unexplored, Foote does seize on another aspect of Twain's personality that greatly intrigued later biographers—his highly developed sense of guilt. There were times when Twain, in a tower of temper, might blame other people for his misfortunes, sometimes without just cause. More often, though, he was piling the blame upon himself, and the thought process could be just as irrational as when he was pointing the finger at someone else. He was always his favorite target.

In the second act of *The Shape of the River*, Foote has the writer erupt with guilt:

> *"First I lose all our money in foolish and willful investments, and I have to tear my family apart and go on a lecture tour to pay off my debts. When it is over, Susy is dead, Jean has her illness which she will have the rest of her life, and now Livy is stricken... Oh, my God. Oh, my God. To have afflicted so those I love."*

Twain had blamed himself when Henry died after the steamboat explosion (he had secured the position for his younger brother). He had blamed himself for Langdon's death (claiming his negligence on a winter's day ride caused the chill that led to the infant's death). And with Livy's health failing, he blamed himself for Susy's death.

He seemed to have spent his life "hunting for a crime he could say he had committed," Kaplan observed in *Mark Twain and His World.* "Even such a casual acquaintance as Mrs. James T. Fields had noted that his whole life was 'one long apology.'"[28]

The constant embracing of guilt may have proven too psychologically demanding for Twain. In the deterministic book *What Is Man?*, published in 1906, he argues that man is a machine driven by his nature, his environment, and his self-interest. There is no such thing as free will, he asserts. Both DeVoto and Kaplan seized on the justification at work behind this grim philosophy. If there is no free will, there can be no blame. "If man is not responsible," DeVoto noted, "then no man can be held responsible. No one, I think, can read this wearisomely repeated argument without feeling the terrible force of an inner cry: Do not blame me, for it was not my fault."[29]

Foote's attempts to give *The Shape of the River* a feel of authenticity is evident throughout the second act. When Twain visits Hannibal in the opening scene, he talks over old times with boyhood chum John Briggs, stopping to tell the town's children a humorous tale. Briggs did see his famous old friend in 1902, and the story is precisely the one attributed to Twain on that day.

Later in the second act, with the family settled in a spacious Riverdale house on the Hudson River, Clara tells Jean that their father's "Christmas story for *Harper's*" was "almost an accurate account of our life here last month when you had pneumonia and we wanted to keep it from Mama." Howells enters, and Jean explains how Clara "had to pretend to Mama I [Jean] was well and happy the whole time I was sick, and invent things for me to be doing every minute of my illness, so Mama would think I was having a busy, useful, happy life." This is again drawn from the accounts set down by Twain, Clara, and others.

The story Clara mentions—"Was it Heaven? or Hell?"—was published in the 1902 Christmas number of *Harper's Magazine.* Readers were touched by the tale of two aged aunts (twins again!) caring for a mother and daughter, both dying. Although piously opposed to lying in all forms, the maiden aunts ply their doomed patients with happy fabrications, and the mother believes her daughter is well.

The story contained a strong dose of prophecy for the Clemens family. A couple of days before that Christmas, Jean fell ill with pneumonia. The doctor had decreed that Livy's heart could bear no upset of any kind, so it fell to Clara to fashion all sorts of lies for her mother. While Jean's fever raged between 103 and 104 for five days, Twain saw "Was it Heaven? or Hell?" enacted in the Riverdale house. Clara's assignment was difficult, but she stood up under Livy's barrage of questions. The mother believed her daughter was well.

Jean's recovery kept prophecy from going any further, but Livy continued to weaken. As *The Shape of the River* poignantly shows, contact with her husband was restricted to brief visits and daily notes.

Matching the thoroughness of Foote's research are the historical touches provided by research consultant Harriet Dryden, art director Edgar Lansbury, and the *Playhouse 90* makeup team. Tone's makeup and costumes are based on pictures of Twain from 1895–96, 1902–04, and 1905–09. When Tone's Twain pauses for a photograph in front of the Hannibal house, it's a close approximation of the famous picture taken in 1902.

The man playing the Hannibal photographer is veteran character actor Len Lesser. He would go on to achieve television fame as Uncle Leo on NBC's *Seinfeld.* Standing next to Lesser in the Hannibal scene are Elizabeth Patterson, best known to TV viewers for playing kindly Mrs. Trumbull on *I Love Lucy*, and Sandy Kenyon, who appeared in several episodes of *The Twilight Zone* and *The Dick Van Dyke Show.*

"It was a pleasure to work with Franchot Tone," Kenyon said. "I always admired him. And I had either worked with a lot of people in that production or would work with them in the future. Shirley Knight and I were in the same acting group at that time. Larry Gates and I were in a *Twilight Zone* that Rod Serling wrote called 'The Shelter,' and we also did a play called *Conversation at Midnight* on Broadway. And then

Nancy Rennick and I were both in the *Twilight Zone* about the airliner trapped in time (Serling's 'The Odyssey of Flight 33'). And then I became one of the favorite actors of Boris Sagal, who directed it. He used me all the time."[30]

Sagal cast Kenyon in "Candidate for Crime," a 1973 *Columbo* mystery he directed, and *A Case of Rape*, the landmark 1974 TV movie starring Elizabeth Montgomery as a rape victim. The director also used Kenyon in the 1963 pilot episode of ABC's *The Travels of Jamie McPheeters*, which starred Dan O'Herlihy and young Kurt Russell. O'Herlihy later played Mark Twain in a sixty-minute PBS drama about the elderly writer reflecting on moments in his life. Titled *Mark Twain: Beneath the Laughter*, it aired on December 15, 1979. Kenyon, by that time, had played the character called Constable Clemens in the 1973 version of *Tom Sawyer*, a big-screen musical starring Johnnie Whitaker, Celeste Holm, and Jodie Foster.

The involvement of Edgar Lansbury, the younger brother of Angela Lansbury, explains the casting of the British actress playing Livy Clemens' nurse. She is stage and screen actress Moyna MacGill, mother of Angela, Edgar, and Bruce Lansbury.

Foote was given a strong hand in the casting for the production, and was present throughout the rehearsal process to answer actors' questions. With sets depicting everything from the decks of ocean liners to the rooms of Stormfield, the production called for some ingenious direction and some tricky shots. A disturbing glimpse of the dead Jean's face underwater lasts mere seconds, but its impact lingers after the final credits.

Almost as impressive as Foote's script is Franchot Tone's moving portrayal of Twain.

"He was really wonderful," Foote said. "He was not our first choice. We got turned down by two or three other people. Fredric March was one of them, and I know we offered it to Hal Holbrook, whose *Mark Twain Tonight!* had been a sensation in New York the year before."[31]

Holbrook, who would win a Tony for the 1966 Broadway run of his celebrated one-man show, doesn't remember seeing the script. "But that was a period when a lot of scripts were being sent to me," he said. "And I had made a decision at that point to turn down offers to play Mark Twain in projects that dramatized his life. I've been sent quite a number of projects like that over the years. I've always turned them down. I suppose it has been my way of protecting the show. I've always been responsible for the words that I put in Mark Twain's mouth."[32]

It was then that someone suggested Franchot Tone. "We hadn't thought of him at first," Foote recalled. "But Franchot was very eager to do a good job. He was quite worried about playing the very emotional scenes. He was worried that, when the cameras were rolling, it wouldn't be there. But it was. He was terribly pleased with his performance. He thought it was some of his best work."[33]

Born Stanislas Pascal Franchot Tone in Niagara Falls, New York, on February 27, 1905, the star received an Oscar nomination for his portrayal of Roger Byam in *Mutiny on the Bounty* (1935). His other notable Hollywood films included *The Lives of a Bengal Lancer* (1935), *Three Comrades* (1938), *Five Graves to Cairo* (1943), and *Phantom Lady* (1944). Mostly cast in second leads in the 1930s and early 1940s, Tone gained respect as an actor with stage work and numerous live television appearances in the 1950s.

He starred in a December 1955 adaptation of Faulkner's *The Sound and the Fury* (not written by Foote) on *Playwrights '56*, and his 1957 New York production of Anton Chekhov's *Uncle Vanya* earned him rave reviews. But Tone's club-hopping lifestyle often landed him in the gossip columns rather than in the theatre section. He was married and divorced four times, and each of his wives was an actress: Joan Crawford (1935–39), Jean Wallace (1941–48), Barbara Payton (1951–52), and Dolores Dorn-Heft (1956–59).

"His private life was kind of silly," Foote conceded. "He was drinking a great deal. But he was very serious about his craft. I must say, I got to know him quite well, and he was really a very serious, very sensitive man. He took his acting very seriously."[34]

Interspersed with marriages, divorces, and acting assignments, there were brawls. In his outstanding book about *The Twilight Zone*, author Marc Scott Zicree tells the story of the anthology series' only episode starring Franchot Tone. Written by Serling and titled "The Silence," it aired on April 28, 1961, only four days short of the date CBS had aired *The Shape of the River* the year before.

Tone didn't show up for the second day of shooting on "The Silence." The director was none other than Boris Sagal. When Tone did show up, Serling, Sagal, and director of photography George T. Clemens were faced with a dilemma—one side of their star's face was a mess of scrapes. Tone claimed he had fallen down a hillside after attending a party. Others said it was a parking lot fight.

With a day's shooting already completed, Serling, Sagal, and Clemens decided to film Tone in profile for the rest of the episode. Cast as a sinister fellow, Tone spoke "out of the corner of his mouth" and with his face "only half-turned," which, according to Zicree, made him seem "predatory and sly." The effect worked so well, as Sagal relates in *The Twilight Zone Companion*, "that at the time a number of critics complimented him on the effect!"[35]

Thirty-year-old John Frankenheimer, just two years away from *The Manchurian Candidate* and *The Birdman of Alcatraz*, was slated to direct *The Shape of the River*. He was a logical choice. Between 1954 and 1960, Frankenheimer had directed a herculean total of 125 TV plays, forty-two of them for *Playhouse 90*. He had been at the helm of the very first episode of *Playhouse 90*, Serling's *Forbidden Area*, which aired on October 4, 1956. And he had directed Foote's adaptation of Faulkner's *Old Man*, which aired on November 20, 1958.

Produced by Coe, *Old Man* was an ambitious undertaking, even by *Playhouse 90* standards. The flood and storm sequences were staged in two huge tanks at Television City. Stars Geraldine Page and Sterling Hayden slogged their way through muddy sets, creating the illusion of two people swamped by the Mississippi River. The 1997 *Hallmark Hall of Fame* remake of the Faulkner story, starring Arliss Howard and Jeanne Triplehorn, won Foote an Emmy.

Other notable *Playhouse 90* productions directed by Frankenheimer included *The Days of Wine and Roses* (with Cliff Robertson), *The Last Tycoon* (with Jack Palance), *For Whom the Bell Tolls* (with Jason Robards), *The Comedian* (with Mickey Rooney), *The Turn of the Screw* (with Ingrid Bergman), *Bomber's Moon* (with future *Shape of the River* cast member Larry Gates in a supporting role), and *The Velvet Alley* (with Katharine Bard).

"I did four shows with Fred Coe, including *Old Man*," Frankenheimer recalled. "But I did all the rest of them for *Playhouse 90* with Martin Manulis as the producer. You know, the year I did *Old Man*, four of the five writers nominated for an Emmy were nominated for *Playhouse 90* dramas I had directed: Horton Foote for *Old Man*, J.P. Miller for *The Days of Wine and Roses*, Rod Serling for *A Town Has Turned to Dust*, and Irving Gaynor Neiman for *Child of Our Time*. And would you believe it? James Costigan won for a *Hallmark Hall of Fame* (*Little Moon of Alban*). But Horton finally got his Emmy for *Old Man* years later. I was supposed to do more for *Playhouse 90*, but I got a movie in 1960."[36]

The film was *The Young Savages*, which was released in 1961. Frankenheimer was immediately replaced on *The Shape of the River* by Sagal, another of TV's finest directors. Born on October 18, 1923, in Dnepropetrovsk, Russia, Sagal's long list of network credits includes the miniseries *Masada* (1981), the 1980 TV movie version of *The Diary of Anne Frank*, and two episodes of Peter Falk's *Columbo* ("The Greenhouse Jungle" and "Candidate for Crime"). He also directed such feature films as Elvis Presley's *Girl Happy* (1965) and Charlton Heston's *The Omega Man* (a 1971 adaptation of Richard Matheson's *I Am Legend*).

He died on May 22, 1981, returning from a trip to scout locations for a TV movie. Exiting a helicopter, he accidentally walked into the tail rotor. His first wife, producer Sara Zwilling, had died of heart disease six years earlier. They had three daughters who would become actresses: Katey Sagal is best known for playing Peg Bundy on Fox's *Married... With Children*, while her younger sisters, twins Jean and Liz, starred in NBC's *Double Trouble*, a 1984–85 situation comedy. One of their two brothers, Joey Sagal, is also an actor. Sagal married his second wife, dancer-actress Marge Champion, in 1977.

"It was the first time I had ever worked with Boris," Foote said. "We were quite fortunate to get him. He had great taste, and he was a gentleman. It was a happy time. We liked each other very much."[37]

Rounding out the Coe team were associate producers Robert Goldman and Russell Stoneham, associate director Lennie Horn, lighting director Tom D. Schamp, technical director Robert Stone, and composer Jerry Goldsmith.

Capturing a wide range of moods, Goldsmith's score punctuates the action without ever overwhelming it. It is at times playful, whimsical, somber, rousing, melancholy, and touching. Goldsmith was another of TV's master artists. Starting with the live dramas of the mid-1950s, he contributed original scores to *Studio One*, *Climax*, *The Twilight Zone*, *Thriller*, *Dr. Kildare*, *The Man from U.N.C.L.E.*, *Barnaby Jones*, and two miniseries—*QB VII* and, reuniting with Sagal, *Masada*. Moving to the big screen, the prolific Goldsmith composed the scores for *Lilies of the Field* (1963), *The Sand Pebbles* (1966), *Planet of the Apes* (1968), *Patton* (1970), *Chinatown* (1974), *The Omen* (1976, for which he won an Oscar), *Star Trek: The Motion Picture* (1979), *Poltergeist* (1982), *Air Force One* (1997), *The Mummy* (1999), and *The Sum of All Fears* (2002).

Tone introduced the *Playhouse 90* episode's storyline out of makeup, then appeared in the first act as Twain approaching sixty. He was hardly recognizable under the makeup, and the actor became even less so as he "aged" more and more effectively as Twain in the next two acts.

"It takes three hours for the makeup," Tone told a newspaper reporter. "I have a new nose, moustache, hair—all that. I couldn't possibly reproduce it without the help of the makeup man."[38]

The length of the makeup procedures for each act ruled out the possibility of a live production. A commercial break between the first and second acts simply wasn't long enough to age Tone from the Twain of 1896 to the Twain of 1902. But once the cameras were in place for each act, the roughly thirty-minute blocks were filmed in sequence.

"We did it all in one shot," said Shirley Knight, who was twenty-two when she played Susy Clemens in *The Shape of the River*. "I started out to be an opera singer, which I believe is why they hired me. I did all my own singing as Susy, who was studying to be a singer. It was like doing a play, where you rehearse for several weeks and then you did it. I had done my share of live dramas by that ltime, so this didn't phase me. And we were very well-prepared, thanks to Boris, who was a very good director, and thanks to Horton, who suggested books we could read. The rehearsal period was a lot of fun, because we all got along so well and we all wanted to do such a good job."[39]

The Shape of the River aired only eleven days after the fiftieth anniversary of Mark Twain's death. A significant endorsement of Tone's portrayal arrived from Elmira, where Twain had piled up so many manuscript pages during those magical summers at Quarry Farm. Greatly impressed with the performance was Ida Langdon, the writer's niece.

"He seemed more like my uncle than any of the Mark Twain impersonators I have seen," she said.[40]

Told of the compliment, Tone gave full credit to Foote, Sagal, and Coe. "If Miss Langdon liked it best," he said, "I am very gratified. It was their teamwork that made it possible."[41]

A little more than five months after the *Playhouse 90* production, Tone was in Elmira to give a lecture on his experiences playing the author of *Tom Sawyer* and *Huckleberry Finn.* Foote also was invited to be part of Elmira College's October 12–14 Mark Twain Festival, but prior commitments kept him from attending.

A Niagara Falls native and a 1927 graduate of Cornell University, Tone was treated as a favorite son by the upstate New York press. "My association with the author is long," he told reporters and photographers greeting him at the airport on the evening of October 13. "I first met Mark Twain at my grandmother's knee."[42]

The next day began with a breakfast interview at the Mark Twain Hotel, followed by a visit to Woodlawn Cemetery, where Tone admired the monument to Twain and placed a wreath of fall leaves at the writer's headstone. Then, with the college's president, Dr. J. Ralph Murray, as his guide, he stepped inside Twain's octagonal study (donated by the Langdon family and moved in 1952 from Quarry Farm to the campus, where it remains today).

With a full-capacity audience of five hundred in attendance, Tone stepped on the stage of the college's Emerson Building auditorium at eight-thirty that night. Titled "An Actor's Approach to Mark Twain," his lecture included readings from *Roughing It* and "The Jumping Frog of Calaveras County." The turning point in his research for the role, Tone told the audience, was his realization that Twain "was a ham at heart." After that, "all I had to do was let the ham in me out."[43]

Tone, who donated his lecture fee back to the college, also revealed that he had worked on Twain's voice by listening to recordings made by the writer's friend, actor William Gillette, and Hal Holbrook. Speaking from "the top of [his] head," he also showed excerpts from *The Shape of the River.* Forty-one years later, excerpts from the *Playhouse 90* production would be shown in the very same auditorium, this time to Twain scholars gathered for the Fourth International Conference on the State of Mark Twain Studies.

"Franchot Tone was an absolute joy to work with," Shirley Knight said of the actor who died in 1968. "I think Franchot was a much a better actor than he may have been given credit for."[44]

Despite Tone's excellent performance, *The Shape of the River* proved to be the next-to-last production for *Playhouse 90*. The anthology series ended its legendary run on May 18 with Rod Serling's *In the Presence of Mine Enemies*, which starred Charles Laughton, Arthur Kennedy, Sam Jaffe, Oscar Homolka, and, cast as a German soldier trying to save a Jewish girl, an unknown youngster named Robert Redford. CBS executive James Aubrey issued the cancellation notice, signaling the end of TV's golden age.

"It really was the end of a wonderful era," Knight said. "Truly creative people were in charge of the medium at that time. It's so much more difficult now to do creative work on television because there are too many people who are not creative who have too much to say. In those days, you didn't even meet with casting directors or network executives. The director, producer, and writer had control."[45]

Knight's second husband, British writer John R. Hopkins, had similarly rewarding experiences when working on scripts for the BBC.

"My husband tried writing for American television," Knight said of Hopkins, whom she married in 1970, "but he eventually said, 'No thank you, I'll write for the BBC.' That was because creative people no longer were in charge. But in the days of live television, you were getting scripts by Horton Foote, Gore Vidal, and Reginald Rose. I really do think some of my best work was done for live television."[46]

One of Foote's favorite actresses, Knight (who was nominated twice for an Oscar in the 1960s and won a 1995 Emmy for her work in HBO's *Indictment: The McMartin Trial*) contends that *The Shape of the River* deserves to be rediscovered because of the insight brought to a major Southern writer of one century by a major Southern writer of another:

"Horton was very intent on showing another side of the man. I certainly didn't realize there were these aspects to Twain before I did *The Shape of the River.* That was a time when we tended to mythicize great American figures like Benjamin Franklin and Mark Twain. And much of Mark Twain is the stuff that myths are made of. I seem to remember that he was born when Halley's Comet was in the sky and died when it had returned. That's the kind of thing that wouldn't be out of place in a myth.

And so is the epic fight back from bankruptcy. But the mythicizing we did before the sixties turned men like Franklin and Twain into jolly one-dimensional figures. Horton gave us someone who ended up being so much more heroic because of the tragedy he faced. The wonderful thing about *The Shape of the River* was that you got the wonderful voices of both Mr. Twain and Mr. Foote. It was a remarkable time."[47]

The riveting and rhythmic blending of these two writers' voices makes *The Shape of the River* remarkable for its time and remarkable forty-three years later.

A Mark Twain Chronology

compiled by Mark Dawidziak

The period of Mark Twain's life covered by Horton Foote's *The Shape of the River* starts in late spring of 1895 and concludes in late December of 1909. Foote, however, has Twain refer to many earlier incidents.

1835: Born Samuel Langhorne Clemens, the sixth child of John Marshall and Jane Lampton Clemens, on November 30 in Florida, Missouri

1838: Brother Henry born on July 13

1839: Sister Margaret dies at age nine on August 17

Family moves to Hannibal, Missouri, where Sam spends his boyhood

1840: Starts attending first Hannibal school in April

1842: Brother Benjamin dies at age nine on May 12

1843: Father, John Marshall Clemens, elected Hannibal's justice of the peace

Spends the first of several consecutive summers on his uncle John Quarles' farm, where he hears stories told by a slave named Uncle Daniel

1845: Takes his first steamboat ride in February to St. Louis

1847: Father dies of pneumonia on March 24

Works for the *Hannibal Gazette* in the fall

1848: Becomes printer's apprentice to Joseph P. Ament of Hannibal's *Missouri Courier*

1849: Formal education ends when he stops attending school in Hannibal

1850: Joins Hannibal's *Western Union*, a newspaper started by his older brother, Orion

1851: First known writing, a sketch about an office fire, appears in *Western Union* on January 16

1853–54: Leaves Hannibal to work as a journeyman "tramp" printer in St. Louis, New York, Philadelphia, and Washington, D.C.

1856: Gives first public speech at a printer's banquet on January 17

1857: Becomes a cub pilot to Horace Bixby in March on a Mississippi River steamboat called the *Paul Jones*

1858: Younger brother, Henry Clemens, dies after June explosion of the steamboat *Pennsylvania*

1859: Receives pilot's certificate on April 9

1861: Joins the Confederate irregulars as a lieutenant, but deserts after two weeks

Heads for the Nevada Territory by overland stage with Orion on July 26

Arrives in Carson City, Nevada, on August 14

1862: Tries mining the Esmeralda claim, about 100 miles south of Carson City, in the Nevada Territory

Sends contributions, signed Josh, to the *Territorial Enterprise*, a newspaper in Virginia City, Nevada

Decides to join the *Territorial Enterprise* in August

1863: For the first time, uses the pen name Mark Twain for February 2 *Enterprise* story

1864: Leaves Virginia City for several newspaper jobs in San Francisco

1865: Tries pocket mining in Angel's Camp, where he hears the "Jumping Frog" story

"Jumping Frog" story is published in *New York Saturday Press* on November 18

1866: Ships for the Sandwich Islands in March as a special correspondent for the *Sacramento Union*

Makes his debut as a humorous lecturer on October 2 in San Francisco

Leaves San Francisco and sails for New York City in December

1867: First book, *The Celebrated Jumping Frog of Calaveras County, and Other Sketches*, is published on May 1

First New York lecture on May 6 at Cooper Union

Leaves on June 8 for a five-month Quaker City excursion to Europe and the Holy Land

Meets Olivia Langdon on December 27

Hears Charles Dickens read on New Year's Eve at New York's Steinway Hall

1868: Visits Hartford, Connecticut, for the first time in January and meets Joseph Hopkins Twichell, pastor of the Hartford Congregational Church (Twichell becomes a lifelong friend)

First season of Lyceum lecture tour opens in Cleveland on November 17

Secretly engaged to Olivia Langdon in November

1869: Formally engaged to Olivia Langdon in February

The Innocents Abroad is published in July by the American Publishing Company

Becomes an owner with a one-third interest in the *Buffalo Express* in August

Starts his second season, 1869–70, on the lecture circuit, on November 1

Meets author-editor William Dean Howells, another lifelong friend, in Boston in November

1870: Marries Olivia Langdon on February 2 in Elmira

Remains in Buffalo, where son, Langdon, is born prematurely on November 7

1871: Small book *Mark Twain's (Burlesque) Autobiography* is published in February

Sells interest in the *Buffalo Express* and moves his family to Hartford in October

Opens third lecture tour season in Bethlehem, Pennsylvania, on October 16

1872: *Roughing It* is published in February

First daughter, Olivia Susan (Susy), born on March 19

Langdon, not yet two, dies on June 2

1873: *The Gilded Age*, a novel written in collaboration with Charles Dudley Warner, is published in December

1874: Sister-in-law Susan Crane builds an octagonal study for him at her home, Quarry Farm, in Elmira, New York, where Twain and his family spend their summers

Second daughter, Clara, born on June 8

The family moves into their new Hartford home, No. 351 Farmington Avenue, in September

First contribution to the *Atlantic Monthly*, "A True Story," appears in November

Tries a typewriter for the first time in December

1875: *Sketches, New and Old* is published in July

1876: Collaborates with Bret Harte on a play, *Ah Sin*

The Adventures of Tom Sawyer is published in December

1877: *Ah Sin* opens in Washington, D.C., on May 7

Makes first trip to Bermuda, with Twichell, in May

Small book *A True Story and the Recent Carnival of Crime* is published in September

1878: Small book of sketches *Punch, Brothers, Punch!* is published in March

Leaves in April for an extended European trip, which includes a walking tour of the Black Forest and the Alps, with Twichell, in August

1880: *A Tramp Abroad* is published in March

1601, a bawdy Elizabethan burlesque, is privately printed and circulated in June

Third daughter, Jane Lampton (Jean), born on July 26

Elmira native Catherine "Katy" Leary is hired by the Clemens family (she remains with them as a maid, housekeeper, seamstress, and nanny for thirty years)

Begins disastrous investing in Paige Typesetting machine

1881: *The Prince and the Pauper* is published in December

1882: Leaves for six-week trip on the Mississippi in April

Small book *The Stolen White Elephant, Etc.* is published in June

1883: *Life on the Mississippi* is published in May

Finishes *Huckleberry Finn* in July

1884: Sets up his niece's husband, Charles L. Webster, as head of his publishing company in May

Begins lecture tour with author George Washington Cable in November

First English edition of *Adventures of Huckleberry Finn* is published in December

1885: Visits Hannibal on January 13

First American edition of *Adventures of Huckleberry Finn* is published in February

Contracts to publish Ulysses S. Grant's *Memoirs* in February (the first volume is published in December)

Susy, thirteen, begins writing her biography of him

1886: Addresses Senate Committee on Copyright on January 28

1888: Receives honorary master of arts degree from Yale University in June

1889: *A Connecticut Yankee in King Arthur's Court* is published in December

1890: Susy Clemens starts Bryn Mawr College in October

Mother, Jane Lampton Clemens, 88, dies on October 27

Jean Clemens has first epileptic seizure in the fall

1891: Charles L. Webster dies on April 26

Due to financial troubles, the family ends its residence in Hartford and sails for France in June

1892: *Merry Tales*, a book of sketches, is published in April by the failing Webster & Co.

The American Claimant is published in May by Webster & Co.

1893: *The 1,000-pound Bank Note and Other New Stories* is published in February

Meets Henry Huttleston Rogers, the Standard Oil executive who will help settle his financial troubles, in September

1894: *Tom Sawyer Abroad* is published in April by Webster & Co.

Enters voluntary bankruptcy hearings for his company on April 18, but resolves to satisfy all debts dollar for dollar

Pudd'nhead Wilson is published in November by former publisher, American Publishing Company

1895: Spends the late spring and early summer in Elmira, preparing lectures at Quarry Farm

Leaves Elmira train station July 14 with Livy and Clara; Susy, Jean, and Katy remain at Quarry Farm

Accompanied by Livy and Clara, he starts his round-the-world lecture tour in Cleveland on July 15

Lectures in Australia and New Zealand in November and December

1896: Lectures throughout India and Ceylon from January to April
Joan of Arc is published in May

Lectures throughout South Africa from May to July

Ends tour in July and sails for England, where a cable tells him that Susy is ill

Susy Clemens, 24, dies of spinal meningitis on August 18 in the Hartford house

Susy Clemens is buried in Elmira's Woodlawn Cemetery on August 23

Tom Sawyer Abroad, Tom Sawyer Detective, and Other Stories is published in November

Settles in England, at 23 Tedworth Square in Chelsea, to work on the round-the-world lecture tour's travel book

Jean's condition is diagnosed correctly as epilepsy

1897: *How to Tell a Story and Other Essays* is published in March

Following the Equator is published in November

Brother, Orion Clemens, dies on December 11

1898: Pays off last creditors in March, less than four years after bankruptcy hearing

Moves in October to Vienna's Hotel Krantz, where the family lives for seven months

1899: Moves to London in October

Literary Essays is published by Harper and Brothers

1900: Settles at Dollis Hill House, near London, in July

The Man That Corrupted Hadleyburg and Other Stories and Essays is published in June

Returns to the United States in October after living in Europe for nine years

Introduces Winston Churchill to his first American lecture audience on December 12

1901: Spends summer at Saranac Lake in upstate New York with Livy, Clara, and Jean

Rents a spacious three-story house in Riverdale on the Hudson River; the family takes up residency there in October, and remains there until July 1903

Receives honorary doctor of laws degree from Yale University on October 20

Meets Albert Bigelow Paine in December

1902: Visits Hannibal for the last time in May, where he sees his childhood friend, John Briggs, and poses in front of his boyhood home

Receives honorary doctor of letters degree from University of Missouri on June 4

Small book *A Double-Barrelled Detective Story* is published

Hires Isabel Lyon as his secretary in November

Story "Was it Heaven? or Hell?" is published in the Christmas number of *Harper's Magazine*

1903: *My Debut as a Literary Person with Other Essays and Stories* is published in April

Hartford home is sold in May

Spends his last summer in Elmira

Ill health of Livy Clemens sends family to live in Florence, Italy, in November

1904: Small book *Extracts from Adam's Diary* is published in April by Harper and Brothers

Olivia Langdon Clemens dies in Florence on June 5

Olivia Langdon Clemens is buried near her children, Langdon and Susy, in Elmira's Woodlawn Cemetery on July 14

Sister, Pamela Clemens Moffett, dies at 72 on August 31

Moves to Manhattan house at 21 Fifth Avenue (corner of Fifth and Ninth Street) in September

Small book *A Dog's Tale* published in September by Harper and Brothers

1905: Spends first summer in Dublin, New Hampshire

Pamphlet *King Leopold's Soliloquy* published in September

Seventieth birthday banquet at Delmonico's on December 5

1906: Starts working with official biographer, Albert Bigelow Paine, in January

Small book *Eve's Diary* is published in June

What Is Man? is privately printed in August

The $30,000 Bequest and Other Stories is published

Appears before House Copyright Committee on December 7

1907: Hosts dinner party for Helen Keller on January 16

Christian Science is published in February

Starts last transatlantic trip to England on June 8

Receives honorary degree from Oxford University on June 26

Small book *A Horse's Tale* is published in October

1908: Moves to new home, Stormfield, in Redding, Connecticut, on June 18

1909: Small book *Is Shakespeare Dead?* is published in April

Removes Isabel Lyon and Ralph Ashcroft from his household and business staff between April and July

Jean Clemens moves into Stormfield on April 26

Henry H. Rogers dies on May 19

Delivers his last public speech on June 9

Is diagnosed with heart disease in July

Small book *Extracts from Captain Stormfield's Visit to Heaven* is published in October

Clara Clemens marries musician Ossip Gabrilowitsch at Stormfield on October 6

Works on "Letters from the Earth" in October and November

Travels to Bermuda with Paine for a month-long stay on November 18

Jean Clemens, 29, dies on Christmas Eve, at Stormfield

Writes "The Death of Jean" in late December

Paine and his family move into Stormfield on December 29

1910: Visits with Howells for the last time on January 5

Sails for Bermuda on January 6

Sails for home, in ill health, on April 12

Clara Clemens and her husband return to Stormfield on April 17

Dies at Stormfield at sunset on April 21

Twichell delivers prayer at April 23 funeral at the Presbyterian Brick Church in New York

Is buried next to Livy, Susy, Jean, and Langdon on April 24 in Elmira, New York

"Let us endeavor so to live that when we come to die even the undertaker will be sorry."

—MARK TWAIN

Pudd'nhead Wilson (1894)

The People and Places in The Shape of the River

These are the significant individuals and places mentioned in *The Shape of the River,* Horton Foote's 1960 *Playhouse 90* drama about the last fifteen years of Mark Twain's life.

The People (in order of appearance):

HENRY HUTTLESTON ROGERS

(January 29, 1840–May 19, 1909):
The Standard Oil director who befriended Mark Twain in the 1890s and structured the plan that allowed the Clemens family to recover from bankruptcy. Although known for his ruthless business practices, Rogers apparently was motivated by his fondness for Twain's writing. He met the author in 1893, earned his complete trust, and became one of his closest friends.

SAMUEL LANGHORNE CLEMENS

(November 30, 1835–April 21, 1910):
The former tramp printer, Mississippi riverboat pilot, prospector, and reporter who, using the pen name Mark Twain, authored such works

as *The Innocents Abroad* (1869), *Roughing It* (1872), *The Adventures of Tom Sawyer* (1876), *The Prince and the Pauper* (1881), *Life on the Mississippi* (1883), *Adventures of Huckleberry Finn* (1884), and *A Connecticut Yankee in King Arthur's Court* (1889). When *The Shape of the River* opens in 1895, Sam Clemens is fifty-nine years old and about to start a round-the-world lecture tour to pay off crippling debts amassed due to poor business investments.

OLIVIA "LIVY" LANGDON CLEMENS
(November 27, 1845–June 5, 1904):
The wife of Mark Twain. Her father, Jervis Langdon, was one of the wealthiest men in Elmira, New York, where she was born. She met thirty-two-year-old Samuel Clemens in late 1867, while attending a New York City reading by Charles Dickens. They were married on February 2, 1870, settling first in Buffalo, then in Hartford. Livy's nickname for her husband was Youth. They had four children—a son, Langdon, who died in June 1872; and three daughters, Susy, Clara, and Jean. She died in Florence, Italy, on June 5, 1904, and Joseph Twichell, their pastor and friend, officiated at the funeral in the same Elmira house where Sam and Livy Clemens had been married.

JANE "JEAN" LAMPTON CLEMENS
(July 26, 1880–December 24, 1909):
The youngest of Sam and Livy Clemens' three daughters. Named for Mark Twain's mother, Jane, she was called Jean by the family. She probably suffered her first epileptic seizure in 1890, although her condition was not correctly diagnosed until 1896. She became her father's private secretary in 1909, dying on December 24 of an apparent heart attack while taking a cold morning bath. Her father poured his emotions into "The Death of Jean," an anguished piece of writing that he said could be the last chapter of his *Autobiography* (see Appendix C).

CATHERINE "KATY" LEARY

(March 17, 1856–October 5, 1934):

The Clemens family's devoted servant, housekeeper, seamstress, and nanny. Born in Elmira, New York, she was hired by Livy Clemens in 1880. She stayed with Susy and Jean Clemens when their parents and sister embarked on the round-the-world lecture tour in 1895, and she was with Susy the following year when she died of spinal meningitis in Hartford. Livy Clemens died in her arms on June 5, 1904. She was also the one who discovered Jean had died on December 24, 1909. And she was present when Twain died on April 21, 1910. Her memories of thirty years with the Clemens family were turned into a book by Mary Lawton, titled *A Lifetime with Mark Twain* (1925).

OLIVIA SUSAN "SUSY" CLEMENS

(March 19, 1872–August 18, 1896):

The oldest of Sam and Livy Clemens' three daughters, believed by many to have been Twain's favorite child. In 1885, at the age of thirteen, she began writing a biography of her famous father. The book remained unfinished, although Twain incorporated segments from it in his sprawling *Autobiography*. The complete text was published in 1985 as *Papa: An Intimate Biography of Mark Twain* (edited by Charles Neider). Susy entered Bryn Mawr in the fall of 1890, but left the school after a year and moved with the family to Europe. She decided to stay in America and pursue her singing lessons when her parents departed for the round-the-world lecture tour in 1895. A year later, about to leave for England with her sister Jean and Katy Leary, she fell ill with a fever. She died on August 18 of spinal meningitis and was buried on August 23 in Elmira's Woodlawn Cemetery.

CLARA LANGDON CLEMENS

(June 8, 1974–November 19, 1962):

The second of Sam and Livy Clemens' three daughters. She accompanied her parents on the 1895 round-the-world lecture tour. An aspiring singer, she married pianist-composer Ossip Gabrilowitsch on October 6, 1909, at her father's last house, Stormfield, near Redding, Connecticut. The only one of Mark Twain's four children to survive him, she was with him when he died on April 21, 1910. She published *My Father: Mark Twain* in 1931. With literary executor Albert Bigelow Paine, she protected the image of Mark Twain by suppressing the darker and more caustic aspects of his writing.

JOHN BRIGGS

(April 18, 1837–July 17, 1907):

One of Mark Twain's boyhood friends in Hannibal, Missouri. It was such childhood pals as Briggs, Will Bowen, Laura Hawkins, Tom Nash, John Garth, Tom Blankenship, and John Lewis Robards who inspired the young characters in *Tom Sawyer* and *Huckleberry Finn*. The character of Ben Rogers is believed to have been modeled on Briggs, the son of a Hannibal businessman. Twain renewed acquaintances with Briggs during his 1902 visit to Hannibal.

WILLIAM DEAN HOWELLS

(March 1, 1837–May 11, 1920):

Eminent American author, critic, poet, essayist, and editor. One of Mark Twain's most cherished friends, he was the one who dubbed Clemens "the Lincoln of our literature." His own novels include *The Rise of Silas Lapham* (1885) and *A Hazard of New Fortunes* (1890). Howells was the assistant editor of *The Atlantic Monthly* when he met Twain in 1869. Twain visited Howells at the magazine's Boston office to thank him for his enthusiastic review of *The Innocents Abroad*. The friendship lasted until Twain's death in 1910. Howells' warm portrait of the writer, *My Mark Twain*, was published in 1910. The letters they exchanged for almost forty years were collected in *Mark Twain–Howells Letters: The Correspondence of Samuel L. Clemens and William Dean Howells, 1872–1910*, a two-volume edition published in 1960, the same year that *The Shape of the River* aired on CBS. Howells' son, John, was the architect who designed Stormfield.

ALBERT BIGELOW PAINE

(July 10, 1861–April 9, 1937):

The novelist, poet, children's author, and biographer who became Mark Twain's literary executor and the first editor of the Mark Twain Papers. Paine met Twain at a 1901 Players Club dinner in New York City. He attended Twain's seventieth birthday dinner in December 1905, and by January 10, 1906, he had obtained Twain's permission to write an authorized biography. From this point, Paine remained a constant presence in Twain's life; between work on the biography (*Autobiography*), there were endless games of billiards. When Jean Clemens died in 1909, Paine and his family moved into Stormfield. Then, when Twain fell gravely ill in Bermuda a few months later, Paine was dispatched to help him home. Paine's three-volume *Mark Twain, A Biography* was published in 1912. He also published several books written by Mark Twain that had not yet been printed, including *The Mysterious Stranger and Other Stories* (1922) and *Mark Twain's Autobiography* (1924), although many of his editorial choices were later called into question by Twain scholars and biographers.

The Places:

HARTFORD, CONNECTICUT:

The city that the Clemens family called home for twenty years. After spending the first year of their marriage in Buffalo, New York, Sam and Livy Clemens moved to Hartford in the fall of 1871. Their infant son, Langdon, died there in June 1872. A large, fanciful house was completed on Farmington Avenue in 1874. It remained their beloved home until 1891, when financial troubles forced the family to move to Europe. Susy Clemens died in the house in 1896, and her mother could never bring herself to enter it again. Twain returned to Hartford for visits in 1900 and 1906. The house was sold in 1903 and today is open to the public.

ELMIRA, NEW YORK:

Livy Clemens' birthplace and summer home to the Clemens family. Although not a location used in *The Shape of the River*, the upstate New York city was Livy Clemens' hometown and is mentioned several times in the *Playhouse 90* drama. It was an important place for the Clemens family. Livy was born there in 1845. She and Mark Twain were married there, in her parents' house, in 1870. And all three of their daughters—Susy, Clara, and Jean—were born there. Starting in 1871, the Clemens family spent almost every summer at Quarry Farm, the home of Livy's sister, Susan Langdon Crane. In 1874, Aunt Sue had an octagonal study built for her brother-in-law on the property, overlooking Elmira, and it was here that many of his greatest books were written. Twain also brought the family to Elmira in 1895 to prepare for the round-the-world lecture tour. He spent his last summer at Quarry Farm in 1903, the year before Livy's death, although his last visit to Elmira was in 1907. Mark Twain, Livy, and their four children are buried in Elmira's Woodlawn Cemetery. In 1952, the study was moved to the Elmira College campus, and the Langdon family donated Quarry Farm to the college in 1983. It is maintained by the Center for Mark Twain Studies, which, every four years, holds a major international conference on the State of Mark Twain Studies.

HANNIBAL, MISSOURI:

The Mississippi River town where Mark Twain lived until the age of seventeen. The Clemens family moved to Hannibal in 1839 when Sam was about to turn four. He lived there until 1853, writing his first known story for a local newspaper in 1851. Twain used Hannibal as the direct model for St. Petersburg, the hometown of Tom Sawyer and Huck Finn. The writer went back to visit Hannibal several times. He lectured there in 1867. He made a three-day stop there in 1882, during a trip to reacquaint himself with the Mississippi River (a journey that impacted both *Life on the Mississippi* and *Huckleberry Finn*). And he visited the town in 1902, when the famous photograph of him posing in front of his boyhood home at 206 Hill Street was taken. The house is open to the public along with a museum run by the Mark Twain Home Foundation.

RIVERDALE, NEW YORK:
A residential community where Mark Twain and his family lived in a rented three-story house on the Hudson River from October 1901 through July 1903. It was here that Livy's fragile health began to fail. The Riverdale area is now a part of the Bronx.

FLORENCE, ITALY:
The city where the Clemens family moved for Livy's health in November 1903. Livy died in a rented villa outside of Florence in June 1904.

DELMONICO'S:
The Manhattan restaurant where Colonel George Harvey, the president of Harper and Brothers publishers and the editor of *Harper's Weekly*, held Mark Twain's seventieth birthday party on December 5, 1905. In attendance were Twain's daughters, Clara and Jean, and his three closest friends—William Dean Howells, Joseph Twichell, and Henry H. Rogers. Also at the celebration were writers George Washington Cable (Twain's traveling companion on his 1884 lecture tour), Richard Watson Gilder, Finley Peter Dunne ("Mr. Dooley"), Willa Cather, George Ade, and Albert Bigelow Paine (soon to become his biographer). Twain delivered a humorous speech on how to be seventy. Harvey appears as a character in *The Shape of the River*, but is given no lines of dialogue.

NEW YORK, NEW YORK:
At the time of the Delmonico's dinner, Twain was living in the rented Manhattan brownstone where he settled after Livy's death. Located at 21 Fifth Avenue (on the southeast corner of Fifth and Ninth), the home is not mentioned in *The Shape of the River*. Twain lived there until 1908. The building was torn down in 1954.

STORMFIELD:

The name given to Mark Twain's final home. Designed by John Mead Howells to resemble an Italian villa, it was built on a hilltop near Redding, Connecticut. Twain moved into the house on Redding Road in June 1908. It was called Stormfield because funds from his story "Captain Stormfield's Visit to Heaven" helped finish the house. Clara was married there on October 6, 1909. Jean died there on December 24, 1909. Mark Twain also died there on April 21, 1910. Another writer with strong Connecticut ties, Eugene O'Neill, unsuccessfully tried to buy Stormfield in the early 1920s. The house burned to the ground in July 1925.

Cast and Credits for the *Playhouse 90* production of

Horton Foote's

The Shape of the River

Aired May 2, 1960, 8–9:30 p.m.,
on the CBS Television Network
Videotaped at Television City, Hollywood

CAST

Samuel Clemens	Franchot Tone
William Dean Howells	Leif Erickson
Livy Clemens	Katharine Bard
Susy Clemens	Shirley Knight
Katy Leary	Katherine Squire
Henry Rogers	Larry Gates
Albert Bigelow Paine	Philip Coolidge
Clara Clemens	Nancy Rennick
Jean Clemens	Jane McArthur
John Briggs	James Bell
Woman at Hannibal	Elizabeth Patterson
Man at Hannibal	Sandy Kenyon
Nurse	Moyna MacGill
Photographer	Len Lesser

Maid	Doris Karnes
Captain	Henry Hunter
Jenny	Sandra Harrison
Conductor	Benny Burt
Doctor	Nelson Olmsted

Producer: Fred Coe
Director: Boris Sagal
Writer: Horton Foote
Music: Jerry Goldsmith
Associate Producers: Robert Goldman, Russell Stoneham
Research Consultant: Harriet Dryden
Associate Director: Lennie Horn
Art Director: Edgar Lansbury
Lighting Director: Tom D. Schamp
Technical Director: Robert Stone

Sponsors:
American Gas Association,
Allstate Insurance Company, Camel cigarettes

the shape of the River

A Play

by Horton Foote

Act 1

FADE IN: MUSIC ROOM OF SAMUEL CLEMENS' HOUSE—DAY.

Lettering on Screen: Hartford, Conn. Late Spring, 1895.

Businessman **HENRY ROGERS**, *Sam's friend, is seated behind a desk talking to* **SAM**. *He has papers before him, which he refers to from time to time.*

ROGERS

Sam, I've had a talk with the creditors of the Webster Publishing Company. I have told them that although there is a serious panic on in America, and businesses are failing everywhere; and creditors taking the assets when there are any, and letting the rest go; and that although the failure of the Webster Publishing House was in no way your fault and you as owner are not legally bound in any way, still you and your wife feel morally responsible to repay your creditors and that you propose to return to the lecture platform and make a tour of the world lecturing and writing a book until you earn every cent they have lost in the business.

SAM

I'm grateful to you, Henry, for your time and the trouble you've taken to help me and my family out of our difficulties.
I don't know how I can repay you...

ROGERS

I want no repayment. But Sam, when this is all over and you have money again, don't invest or sign contracts without consulting me or someone who knows about business. I have just been studying the patents and schemes of the business you've lost money in and I…

SAM

I know. I know. I pray now I've learned my lesson.

ROGERS

I'm sure you have. I know it's been a very difficult time for you.

SAM

It has. But I'm recovering from the first terrible shock. When I was a boy and was trying to learn how to be a pilot on the river I asked Mr. Bixby, my teacher, if when I had learned the shape of the river in the 500,000 different ways he was demanding in asking of me to learn it, would it stay the same, would it keep the same form and not go fooling around. Well I soon found out it didn't. To be a river pilot you had to learn more than any man ought to know and you had to learn it all over again in a different way every twenty-four hours, and I have found that to be a practice throughout my life. Every time I get used to something, get comfortable in a way of living and I think I've learned all the things that I need to know, I have to start in learning all over again and figure out a new way to do and get along. I tell you, Henry, "all through my life I have been the easy prey of the cheap adventurer. He came, he lied, he robbed and went his way and the next one arrived by the next train and scraped up what was left. Instead of sticking to what I know, I have to try every fool scheme that comes along, that gives promise of sudden riches." My wife has made out a strict budget for us here.

(**ROGERS** *hands him paper*)

She says with the money from the tour and from the book I intend writing and if we live in the summers in Europe, economizing every way, we can pay off our debts in four years.

ROGERS

You realize, Sam, you owe over $100,000.

SAM

Yes, sir, but you see.... How long do you think it will take?

ROGERS

You can have as many years as you want. Let's say seven to start with.

SAM

Seven.... Well, you may be right...

ROGERS

Will your family go on the world tour with you?

SAM

Only my wife and Clara.

ROGERS

Now which is the oldest girl?

SAM

Susy. She'll stay here on a farm building up her strength, and then she will go to Paris and prepare for opera.

ROGERS

And Jean is your youngest child?

SAM

Yes. She will stay here with her nurse and go on with school. We've never been separated before as a family for any length of time, but we know it must be done.

(Starts out of his room)

I have told the manager of the tour that all money is to be sent to you.

ROGERS

Thank you. I will send you and Mrs. Clemens your money each month for your living expenses. I will bank the rest. I have told the creditors they will all be paid off at the same time.

SAM

Thank you.

(They shake hands)

In God We Trust. All others pay cash.

DISSOLVE TO: HALLWAY.

Trunk with label marked "Mr. and Mrs. Samuel Clemens, Vancouver, B.C." LIVY *at upstage trunk.* JEAN *comes down the steps.*

LIVY

Jean, run up to my bedroom and see if I left any linens there.

JEAN

Yes…

She starts up the stairs.

LIVY

And you might ask Katy if she knows of any last things to be packed.

JEAN

Yes, Ma'am…

She goes hurrying out. KATY *comes in from the back kitchen.*

KATY

What are you doing, Mrs. Clemens?

LIVY

Just some last rearranging, Katy.

KATY

Why didn't you call me?

LIVY

Well, since I'm going to be in charge of packing and repacking all these trunks for the next eight months, I think I'd better get used to it. I sent Jean up to look for some linens. Will you go see if she's found them?

KATY

Yes, Ma'am.

She starts up the stairs.

LIVY

And bring anything else you see to go. And tell Mr. Clemens if he has anything to send it on.

KATY

I will.

She goes up the stairs. SUSY *comes in from the music room.*

SUSY

May I help you, Mama?

LIVY

Oh, Susy, no thank you. Katy and Jean are helping me.

SUSY

Where is Clara?

LIVY

She should be home very soon now. She went into town to do some shopping for herself.

SUSY

All right then, I'll be in the music room if you want me.

She goes. SAM *comes down the stairs.*

LIVY

Youth, did Katy find you?

SAM

Yes, I have nothing else to pack.

(He holds up a copy book he carries)

Look what I came across in my study when I was going through my papers—the biography that Susy started about me.

*(*SUSY *begins to sing in the music room. He crosses to door.)*

Susy has been given a beautiful voice, Livy…

LIVY

Yes, she has.

SAM

You know, Livy, I honestly believe that Susy is more like me than any of the children.

LIVY

Do you, Youth?

SAM

I do. I don't mean I love her any more than the others, but I see myself more in her. I've always hoped that some day she will finish this.

LIVY

Well, I don't think she will now.

SAM

She might, Livy…

LIVY

I don't think so, Youth. She's 23 now. All she thinks about is studying her voice. All of her interests are in music now. I think she loves music better than anything else in the world.

SAM

Well, maybe you're right. It is selfish of me, I suppose, to want her to go on with it.

(He opens up the copy book. He reads.)

I was fifty the year she began this and she was thirteen. That's right, isn't it?

LIVY

Yes.

SAM

"We are a very happy family. We consist of Mama, Papa, Jean, Clara and me. It's Papa I'm writing about and I sure have no trouble in not knowing what to say about him as he is a very striking character... Papa uses very strong language but I have an idea not nearly as strong as when he first married Mama... He doesn't like to go to church at all. Why, I never understood until just now. He told us just the other day that he could not bear to hear anyone talk but himself, but that he could listen to himself talk for hours without getting tired. Of course, he said this as a joke, but I have no doubt it was founded on truth."

(He closes the book)

Those were happy days for all of us, Livy. I wonder if we'll ever have such happy times together again?

LIVY

Of course we will, Youth.

(SUSY enters)

Now you have to forgive me while I finish this packing.

SAM

I could hear you singing, Susy. It was beautiful.

SUSY

Thank you, Papa.

SAM

Guess what I have here. A copy of the biography you were writing of me.

SUSY

Where did you find that? I thought I had torn it up.

SAM

I had hidden it away.

SUSY

Let me see it.

She tries to get it from him. They playfully struggle over the book. **SAM** *holds on to it.*

SAM

No. No.

SUSY

Let me see it.

SAM

What are you going to do with it?

SUSY

Never mind. I don't want people looking at it.

SAM

No, I'm going to keep it. It means a great deal to me.

SUSY

Now you give that back to me. Well, all right.

SAM

Do you promise to take good care of yourself while we are gone, Susy?

SUSY

Yes, Papa. I'm going to be so robust and strong after my year on the farm that you won't know me after you come back.

JEAN *and* KATY *come down the stairs with some linens.*

KATY

Now, this is everything, Mrs. Clemens.

LIVY

Thank you.

She takes them. CLARA *comes in the front door.*

SAM

Hello, Clara.

CLARA

Hello, Papa.

LIVY

Clara, did you get your camera fixed?

CLARA

Yes, Mama. I also got some more talcum powder.

LIVY

More?

JEAN *crosses in.*

CLARA

I'll pack it, Mama. The driver wants to know what time you want the carriage tonight, Papa, to take us to the station.

SAM

At six thirty.

KATY

I'll go tell him.

She goes.

SAM

Well, Clara, at 12:30 tonight, you and your mother and me will be on our way around the world.

(The three girls instinctively go up close to him)

I made up my mind to one thing. After these debts are paid off, I'm bringing us all back here and we will never leave again. Your Mama says we can be free of debt in four years, but Mr. Rogers says it will be at least seven, but I'm going to work as hard as I can and if it's humanly possible to be rid of them in three years, I'm going to do it. But there's one thing, Livy—on the lecture platform I'm going to have to go back to my native twang and you're just going to have to put up with it.

JEAN

Papa you never did get rid of it.

SAM

Well, let us say that I shall exaggerate my failure.

LIVY

Now, it doesn't matter about that, Youth. We're going to all meet in England next summer and we'll be together there for awhile; these first ten months will go very fast.

(LIVY *goes to* SUSY)

Susy, sing for us. That will cheer us all up.

SUSY

You sing for us, Papa.

SAM

Nobody likes to hear me sing but you, Susy…

JEAN

That's not fair, Papa.

CLARA

We love to hear you sing.

SAM *starts out to the music room. The others follow.*

INT: MUSIC ROOM—DAY.

SAM *enters followed by the others. He goes to the piano. He sits down at the piano to play. He clears his throat many times before he begins and then sings quite loudly with his head thrown back and his eyes fixed on the ceiling.*

SAM

(Singing)

"Rise, shine, give God
The Glory, Glory."

EXT: STATION—NIGHT.

It is 12:30 at night. The CLEMENS *family are on the platform, bidding farewell to each other. The* CONDUCTOR *calls: "All Aboard."* CLARA, SAM CLEMENS, LIVY CLEMENS *hug and kiss* JEAN *and* SUSY *and tell them goodbye.* CLARA *embraces* KATY.

CLARA

Goodbye, Katy.

KATY

Goodbye, Darlin'.

(SAM *and* LIVY *shake* KATY'S *hand)*

Goodbye, Mrs. Clemens. Goodbye, Mr. Clemens.

SAM & LIVY

Goodbye, Katy.

KATY

I'll take good care of Jean and Susy now, so don't worry.

CLARA, **LIVY**, *and* **SAM** *board the train, leaving* **SUSY**, **JEAN**, *and* **KATY** *on the platform.* **CLARA** *goes inside.* **SAM** *and* **LIVY** *remain on the steps.*

SAM

Don't cry, Livy, please don't cry. We'll all be together again before long.

They go into their compartment. He holds his wife and they continue waving goodbye. **CLARA** *stands off to one side waving goodbye to her sisters.*

FADE IN: MONTAGE.

1. TRAIN—WHEELS
2. MAP—WORLD TOUR
3. POSTER

SAM

Few of us stand prosperity, another man's I mean.

AUDIENCE REACTION

4. TRAIN
5. MAP
6. POSTER

SAM

Often the surest way to convey misinformation is to tell the truth.

AUDIENCE REACTION

7. TRAIN
8. MAP
9. POSTER

DISSOLVE TO: CONCERT HALL.

SAM *walks in. Applause.*

SAM

Being told I would be expected to talk here, I inquired what sort of talk I ought to make. They said it should be something suitable to youth—something didactic, instructive, or something in the nature of good advice. Very well. I have a few things on my mind, which I have often longed to say for the instruction of the young; for it is in one's tender, early years that such things will best take root and be most enduring and most valuable. First then I will say to you, my young friends, and I say it beseechingly, urgently—Always obey your parents, when they are present.

(Mild laugh)

This is the best policy in the long run, because if you don't, they will make you.

(Bigger)

Most parents think they know better than you do, and you can generally make more by humoring that superstition than you can by acting on your own better judgment. Be respectful to your superiors, if you have any,

(Big)

also to strangers, and sometimes to others. If a person offends you, and you are in doubt as to whether it was intentional or not, do not resort to extreme measures; simply watch your chance and hit him with a brick.

(Roar)

That will be sufficient. If you shall find that he had not intended any offense, come out frankly and confess yourself in the wrong when you struck him; acknowledge it like a man and say you didn't mean to.

(Applause)

Leave dynamite to the low and unrefined. Go to bed early, get up early—this is wise.

(Crosses downstage left)

But, of course, the best thing to get up with is a lark. It gives you a splendid reputation with everybody to know that you get up with a lark;

(Laugh)

And if you get the right kind of lark, and work at him right, you can easily train him to get up at half past nine every time—it is no trick at all.

Laugh and applause. SAM *lights a cigar.*

DISSOLVE TO: MONTAGE.

1. TRAIN

2. MAP

DISSOLVE TO: MUSIC ROOM.

SUSY, JEAN, *and* KATY *are there, seated at piano.* SUSY *is reading a letter.*

SUSY

"Dear Susy: Happy 24th Birthday. We are in India now. Played Calcutta February 12 to a packed house, and every day brings us closer to paying off these debts and if I see anyone approaching who looks like he is even anticipating asking me to invest in a business, I run from him like he has the plague. Your mother and I are counting the days before we will be all together in England for the summer."

DISSOLVE TO: MONTAGE.

1. AUDIENCE REACTION

2. TRAIN

3. MAP

DISSOLVE TO: LECTURE HALL.

SAM *standing on platform. Applause.*

SAM

Never handle firearms carelessly. The sorrow and suffering that have been caused through the innocent but needless handling of firearms by the young! Once, right in the next farm house where I was spending the summer, a grandmother, old and gray and sweet, one of the loveliest spirits in the land, was sitting at her work, when her young grandson crept in and got down an old battered, rusty gun which had not been touched for many years and supposed not to be loaded, and pointed at her, laughing and threatening to shoot. In her fright she ran screaming and pleading toward the door on the other side of the room; but as she passed him he placed the gun almost to her very breast and pulled the trigger! He had supposed it was not loaded. And he was right—it wasn't.

(Big laugh)

So there wasn't any harm done. It is the only case of that kind I ever heard of.

(Small laugh)

Therefore, just the same, don't you meddle with old, unloaded firearms. They are the most deadly and unerring things that have ever been created by man. You don't have to rest, you don't have to have any sights on the gun, you don't have to take aim, even. No, you just pick out a relative and bang away, and you are sure to get him.

(Big laugh)

A youth who cannot hit a cathedral at thirty yards with a Gatling Gun in three-quarters of an hour, can take up an old empty musket and bang his grandmother every time, at a hundred.

(Big laugh)

The very thought of it makes one shudder.

Applause. He lights a cigar.

Audience reaction.

DISSOLVE TO: MUSIC ROOM.

SUSY *is there looking at some music.* KATY *comes in with a cablegram.*

KATY

Here's a cablegram from your Mama and Papa. They've arrived in England and they've rented a house for the summer and they're anxious to see us.

*(*KATY *hands the cablegram to* SUSY *and sits)*

I think we should go to New York tonight and stay in a hotel and get a good sleep, before taking the boat tomorrow.

SUSY

Katy, can we wait here tonight?

KATY

Why?

SUSY

I don't know. I don't feel like traveling. I don't know what's wrong. I'm sure if I rest this evening…

KATY

Miss Susy, do you have a temperature?

SUSY

I don't think so.

KATY

I think you do. I don't think you look well, Miss Susy. I think I'd better call a doctor.

SUSY

I'll be all right, Katy.

KATY

Of course you will be. But you lie down here and I'll call a doctor.

(SUSY cries)

What is it, Miss Susy?

SUSY

I don't know. I don't feel well.

KATY holds SUSY close to her.

DISSOLVE TO: COTTAGE.

A room in the Clemens cottage in England. LIVY comes in with a cablegram.

LIVY

Youth, we've received a very mysterious letter from Katy saying that Susy is not feeling well, and that they have had to postpone sailing for a week.

(She hands the letter to him. He rises.)

What do you make of that?

SAM

I don't know, but try not to worry. Katy is very reliable. If anything were seriously wrong she would tell us.

LIVY

I know, but I'm concerned. I think I'll cable them back immediately, and ask for particulars.

(She starts out)

And we'd better check on boats, in case I have to go to her.

SAM

All right, Livy.

CLARA *comes in.*

CLARA

Mama, a cable has just arrived. It says that Susy can't leave in a week. It says that although her recovery is certain, it will be long.

LIVY *takes the cablegram. She reads it and then hands it to* **SAM**.

LIVY

Youth, I think Clara and I should go to America at once.

SAM

All right, Livy. I'll go see about passage. You and Clara begin your packing.

He goes out of the room.

DISSOLVE TO: SUSY'S BEDROOM.

She's in bed. She is suffering from fever. A raging fever. She gets out of bed. She starts to sing. It's an operatic aria. She begins to dress herself. **KATY** *comes running in.*

KATY

Miss Susy, what are you doing out of bed? Get back in bed, please. Please!

(**SUSY** *continues singing, even though she allows* **KATY** *to lead her back to bed)*

Your Mama and Miss Clara sailed yesterday. They're on their way to you.

SUSY

Mama's dead.

KATY

No, no, she's not, Miss Susy. She is on her way to you. All right, darling, all right. Lie down in bed now. Lie down, Susy.

SUSY *breaks away from her. She goes across the room. She begins her singing again.*

SUSY

Up go the trolley cars for Mark Twain's daughter. Down go the trolley cars for Mark Twain's daughter.

(Again she begins to sing. She breaks off suddenly, screaming.)

I'm blind. I'm blind.

KATY

Sh… Sh…

KATY *gets her into bed.* **SUSY** *lies down.* **KATY** *covers her up.*

SUSY

Help me! Help me!

KATY

I'll help you, darling. I'll help. Just try to be quiet.

SUSY

I'm blind. I'm blind—you're blind.

(She whimpers like a child. She takes her hand and feels **KATY'S** *face.)*

Mama. Mama.

KATY *screams.*

DISSOLVE TO: CAPTAIN'S OFFICE.

The **CAPTAIN** *is there. There is a knock at door.*

CAPTAIN

Come in.

CLARA *comes in.*

CLARA

You wanted to see me, sir?

CAPTAIN

Yes. I've very sad news for you and your mother. When our ship docked this morning this was brought to us.

(He hands her a newspaper)

I thought it best, if you told her.

Headline: "Mark Twain's eldest daughter dies of spinal meningitis."

DISSOLVE TO: STATEROOM.

The suitcases are packed and ready for unloading. LIVY CLEMENS *is there.* CLARA *comes in.* LIVY *looks up and sees her standing there.*

LIVY

I don't believe it. I don't believe it. I don't believe it. I don't believe it.

CLARA *nods her head and runs to her mother.* LIVY *holds her.*

DISSOLVE TO: CLOSE SHOT—SAM.

SAM

Many a time I said the two most pathetic moving things to me in the English tongue are these—one is a refrain of a long ago forgotten story familiar to me in my earliest boyhood—"In the days when we went gypsying a long time ago," and the other, "Departed this life."

DISSOLVE TO: GRAVESTONE.

Headstone is carved: Susan Clemens, Born March 19, 1872, Died August 18, 1896.

SAM

(V.O.)

"Warm summer sun shine brightly here. Warm southern wind blow softly here. Green sod above lie light, lie light, Good night, dear heart, good night, good night."

Act 2

EXT: HANNIBAL HOUSE—DAY.

Lettering on Screen: Hannibal, Mo.—The Boyhood Home of Sam Clemens. Spring, 1902.
A crowd of people is in the yard and along the sidewalk in front of the house. On the ground, at the steps of the house, are photographers. A WOMAN *makes her way through the crowd and stops by a* MAN *waiting in the crowd.*

WOMAN

Excuse me.

(She crosses through)

Excuse me. Is this the house Mark Twain lived in as a boy?

MAN

Yes, Ma'am.

WOMAN

What time is he due here?

MAN

Paper said sometime this morning.

WOMAN

That's what I was told.

MAN

He's been in Europe you know.

WOMAN

Is that so?

MAN

Oh, yes. Europe and India and I don't know where all. He was over there, it said in the paper, paying off a raft of debts.

WOMAN

I declare.

MAN

He's coming back this way to accept a degree from the University of Missouri.

Another MAN *passes through. Says hello.*

WOMAN

Are you a native of Hannibal?

MAN

Yes, Ma'am.

WOMAN

Did you ever know him?

MAN

Oh, no Ma'am. He was gone from here a long time before I was born.

WOMAN

(Laughing)

Yes, of course.

(Another MAN *passes through. Says hello.)*

I rode fourteen miles to get a look at him.

MAN

Is that so?

WOMAN

I think what he writes is comical. Don't you?

MAN

Yes, I do.

WOMAN

This is the first trip he's made back home in a long time, isn't it?

MAN

Yes'm.

SAM CLEMENS, *accompanied by* JOHN BRIGGS, *comes along the street. The crowd makes way for them, and he and* JOHN BRIGGS *walk through the yard, up to the steps of the house.*

WOMAN

Oh, there he comes. Isn't that him?

MAN

Yes'm. I believe so.

WOMAN

Oh, he looks much older than I expected and sadder, too. Why, he doesn't look comical at all.

MAN

No'm, I wouldn't say so. Oh, that's our John Briggs. He lives here in Hannibal. He grew up with Mark Twain. Hi, John.

JOHN

Oh, hello there. Is it like you remember, Sam?

SAM

No, the yard is different. The trees are gone. The whole street's different. The town, too, for that matter. I don't know what I expected it to do, stand still for me, I reckon. The fence I whitewashed is over there.

PHOTOGRAPHER

Mr. Clemens, will you stand for a moment in the doorway of your house? We want to take your picture.

SAM

All right, young fella.

(The **PHOTOGRAPHER** *poses* **SAM** *in the doorway)*

I understand John Robards and Ed Pierce are still living here.

JOHN

Yes they are. And Buck Brown. He was your rival once, you remember, in a spelling contest in which you beat him, I believe.

SAM

I could always spell if I couldn't do nothin' else.

*(***MAN*** yells from crowd: Say a few words to us* **SAM***)*

I will as soon as these persevering, persistent photographers finish with me.

The **PHOTOGRAPHER** *takes his picture.*

PHOTOGRAPHER

We are through with you now, Mr. Clemens.

SAM

Thank you.

(He walks to the edge of the porch and makes his speech)

I see there are a lot of boys and girls here this morning. Little boys and girls I want to tell you a story which illustrates the value of perseverance—sticking to your work, as it were. When I was a little boy in Hannibal, I used to play a good deal up there on Holliday's Hill, which of course you all know.

(He points to JOHN *beside him)*

John Briggs and I played up there. I don't suppose there are any little boys as good as we were then, but of course, that is not to be expected. Little boys in those days were 'most always good little boys, because those were the good old times when everything was better than it is now, but never mind that. Well, once upon a time, on Holliday's Hill, they were blasting out rock, and a man was drilling for a blast. He sat there and drilled and drilled and drilled perseveringly, until he had a hole down deep enough for the blast. Then he put in the powder and tamped and tamped and tamped it down, but maybe he tamped it a little too hard, for the blast went off and he went up into the air, and we watched him. He went up higher and higher and got smaller and smaller. First he looked as big as a child, then as big as a dog, then as big as a kitten, then as big as a bird, and finally he went out of sight. John Briggs was with me, and we watched the place where he went out of sight, and by and by we saw him coming down—first as big as a bird, then as big as a kitten, then as big as a dog, then as big as a child, and then he was a man again, and landed right in his seat and went on drilling—just persevering, you see, and sticking to his work. Little boys and girls, that's the secret of success. Just like that poor but honest workman on Holliday's Hill. Of course you won't always be appreciated. He wasn't. His employer was a hard man, and on Saturday night when he paid him, he docked him fifteen minutes for the time he was up in the air—but never mind, he had his reward.

The people are in a storm of enjoyment when he finishes. They applaud. SAM *and* JOHN *start inside the house.*

JOHN

I'm so glad you were able to stop by Hannibal on your way to the University, Sam.

INT: HOUSE—DAY.

SAM *enters followed by* JOHN.

SAM

I wouldn't have missed coming here for the world.

JOHN

Are you happy to be living in America again?

SAM

Yes, I am, John. I was some three years paying off these debts, but that's done and behind me now.

JOHN

You went all over the world, didn't you?

SAM

All over. Once there was a letter sent to me addressed: Mark Twain, "God knows where." And it reached me too.

MOVING SHOT AS SAM AND JOHN WALK THROUGH THE HOUSE.

JOHN

Do either of your daughters share your talent for writing?

SAM

No. My daughter, Clara, is interested, like Susy was, in music. And my youngest daughter, Jean, is learning to typewrite. She helps me with my manuscripts.

JOHN

I'm sorry to hear that Mrs. Clemens isn't well, Sam.

SAM

She's never been strong, John. When she was a girl of sixteen she had an accident from which she never fully recovered. And recently she has been tiring herself a great deal. You see, my wife has the spirit of a steam engine and a frame of flesh, and she's continually wracking that frame with a tireless industry. Anyway, about three weeks ago, I was awakened one morning by a cry. I saw my wife standing on the opposite side of the room leaning against the wall for support and panting. She said to me, "I'm dying," and I thought she was. I helped her back to the bed and sent for our doctor. He said it was a nervous breakdown and nothing but absolute rest, seclusion, and only careful nursing could help her. My daughter, Clara, is with her constantly. Jean and I are not permitted to enter her room.

(He takes out a cigar and lights it)

I suppose it's just as well. I don't think I should go in to see her even if the doctor permitted it. For I would sure come out with some startling yarn that would make the hair of a wolf stand on end.

(Stops on landing)

I don't know if you knew, but my daughter, Jean, has suffered epilepsy since Susy's death. I know that worries her mother constantly.

(They enter a very small room)

It all seems too small to me, John. A boy's home is a big place to him. I suppose if I should come back again ten years from now, it would be the size of a bird house. This was my bedroom.

(Crosses to window)

It's almost sixty years since I climbed down that rain pipe.

(Sits)

Almost sixty years.

DISSOLVE TO: SEWING ROOM.

Lettering on Screen: The Clemens House, Riverdale, N.Y.

There has been a recent snow storm and outside the trees and the yard are covered with snow and ice. JEAN *is typing away.* CLARA *is reading.* KATY *comes in.*

KATY

Mr. Howells is here.

CLARA

Oh good. Have him come up...and Katy you'd better tell Father.

KATY

I will.

She goes.

JEAN

(Rising)

There. That's done.

CLARA

You know that Christmas story for *Harper's* is almost an accurate account of our life here last month when you had pneumonia and we wanted to keep it from Mama.

JEAN

And I thank you for taking such good care of us, Clara.

CLARA

Oh, nonsense...

JEAN

I do. I don't know what any of us would do without you.

CLARA

You'd manage.

JEAN

I'm sorry you've had to give up going into New York for your voice lessons this winter.

CLARA

(Rising)

I'll start again, soon.

JEAN

It must be wonderful to have a talent like you have and Susy had.

CLARA

Maybe you have a talent, too, and you'll discover it some day.

JEAN

No. I have no talent. That's why I'm glad to be learning practical things like typing and secretarial work.

HOWELLS *comes in.*

HOWELLS

Hello, young ladies.

CLARA

Oh, Mr. Howells.

JEAN

Hello, Mr. Howells.

HOWELLS

How well you're looking, Jean. I expected to find an invalid.

JEAN

I'm feeling fine now.

CLARA

But she was very ill, Mr. Howells, and we were concerned about her.

JEAN

I think Clara will be a great actress some day, Mr. Howells. She had to pretend to Mama I was well and happy the whole time I was sick, and invent things for me to be doing every minute of my illness, so Mama would think I was having a busy, useful, happy life.

HOWELLS

And she was never suspicious?

JEAN

Not once, was she, Clara?

CLARA

No, but I'm glad it's behind me. Father's waiting outside Mother's room, hoping to see her for a few minutes this morning. Katy has gone to tell him you're here.

(She starts out of the room)

I'll go see about our lunch.

HOWELLS

Thank you.

JEAN

Father said you could read this story if you wanted to.

HOWELLS

I'd like to...thank you.

He takes the manuscript and begins to read. JEAN *starts out of the room.*

JEAN

Just make yourself comfortable. He'll be along shortly.

DISSOLVE TO: LIVY'S BEDROOM.

LIVY *is in bed.* NURSE *crosses to her from window.*

LIVY

It's a great comfort for me having the river to watch. When is Mr. Clemens coming to see me?

NURSE

After the doctor's visit.

LIVY

Mr. Howells is coming to visit Youth today. I'm so glad he's to have some company.

NURSE

Isn't Mr. Howells a writer too?

LIVY

Yes, a very distinguished one, and one of Mr. Clemens' oldest friends...

There is a knock at the door. The **NURSE** *goes. She opens it. The* **DOCTOR** *is there.*

NURSE

Come in, Doctor.

The **DOCTOR** *comes into the room.*

LIVY

Hello, Doctor.

DOCTOR

Hello, Mrs. Clemens. How are you today?

LIVY

Very well, thank you.

DOCTOR

Excuse me for a moment.

He goes to her beside and takes her pulse. He looks at her for a moment and then goes over to the **NURSE** *by the window. He whispers something to her and she goes out of the room.*

INT: FOYER—DAY.

SAM *is seated outside the door. The* NURSE *comes out. He rises.*

NURSE

The Doctor asked me to tell you he thinks it best if you didn't see Mrs. Clemens for the next three days.

SAM

Is she worse?

NURSE

I don't think so. I just think he wants her to have absolute quiet.

SAM

Don't you think my not coming will concern her and make her think she's getting worse?

NURSE

Perhaps at first, but then I'm sure finally she will understand it is only for her good.

SAM

All right.

(He reaches in this pocket and takes out a piece of paper)

I wrote this note for her to have in case I couldn't see her. Do you want to read it and see if it's all right for her to see? It's just a little something to amuse her.

NURSE

I think it is all right to give her.

SAM

Thank you.

SAM *starts away.*

INT: THE SEWING ROOM—DAY.

HOWELLS *is there reading the story when* SAM *comes in.*

SAM

Welcome to Riverdale.

HOWELLS

(Rising)

Sam…

SAM

It was nice of you to come all this way. I told the girls I don't like to leave here while there is a chance I might see Livy, but my visits with her are necessarily so short.

HOWELLS

How is Livy this morning?

SAM

Yesterday when I saw her she seemed so well, but today they won't let me visit her. When I was lecturing in India I heard a legend of one of their Emperors that they revered. When his son fell ill with fever, he walked around the boy's bed three times and said, "I have bourn it away," and he did bear it away. The fever left his son and came to him instead and he died. I have walked around Livy's bed many times saying to myself, "I have bourn it away" but she lies there suffering and I am here.

(He sees the manuscript)

Have you been reading that?

HOWELLS

Oh, yes. Jean told me I might. Well, I'm glad you're able to write again, Sam.

SAM

I'm not writing. I'm working, and I work eight, nine, ten hours a day.

HOWELLS

But Jean tells me you have written a great deal.

SAM

I've started a great deal.

(Sits)

I'll tell you the truth. In the last six weeks I have started sixteen things wrong. Three books and thirteen magazine articles, and could only make two small things, fifteen hundred words altogether, succeed. And I tell you this. I haven't done much better in the months and years since Susy's death. Some things, it's true, I never intended finishing. But others I wanted badly to complete, and I don't know how. Sometimes I want desperately to finish them, but I always fail.

HOWELLS

Sam, you're distressed and worried and overwrought. You must be patient with yourself. I'm your old friend. I know your nature. I know your moods. I've seen you this way before, Sam. There's hardly been a time in the last thirty years that you haven't had two or more unfinished manuscripts lying around. I heard you say that you stopped in the middle of *Tom Sawyer* and let it alone for two years and then one day took it out, read the last chapter you had written and then went on again. And you wrote to me in the middle of *Huck Finn* that you could not go on, and that you might burn it. I've heard you say many times that when the tank went dry that you've only to leave it alone and it will fill up again while you're asleep. Wasn't there a two-year lapse before *The Prince and the Pauper* was finished?

SAM

Yes.

HOWELLS

And *A Connecticut Yankee?*

SAM

Yes. With one difference. Then I wanted to write well. I write now because it's the only work I know, but I don't care about it. I want to see my wife get well, and I want to find the way to heal her broken heart.

HOWELLS

I know that Sam, but...

SAM

Listen to me...

HOWELLS

I will not have you go on this way, punishing yourself...

SAM

Listen to me. I have to tell you... Sometimes I am afraid that I have done something to bring all this about, that I am being punished.

HOWELLS

Sam...

SAM

Listen to me, please. First I lose all our money in foolish and willful investments, and I have to tear my family apart and go on a lecture tour to pay off my debts. When it is over, Susy is dead, Jean has her illness which she will have the rest of her life, and now Livy is stricken... Oh, my God. Oh, my God. To have afflicted so those I love. Livy feels when she's stronger we should go to Italy and live. We were happy when we were living there before. She loved Italy, and the people and the climate, and the girls did. Maybe if we can get back there, it will be better for us...

KATY comes into the room.

KATY

Miss Clara asked me to tell you that your lunch is ready.

HOWELLS

Thank you.

SAM

You go on. I'll join you. I want to write another little note to Livy, so she'll have it this afternoon. It's all she has to occupy her.

HOWELLS

(Rising)

All right.

He goes on out. SAM *goes to the desk.*

SAM

(Speaks as he writes)

Another note, my Dear. I've just looked outside. The naked tree branches are tear-beaded, and nature has the look of trying to keep from breaking down and sobbing, poor old thing. I feel so full of hope for us.

(There is a knock on the door)

Come in.

The DOCTOR *comes in.*

DOCTOR

Mr. Clemens, Mrs. Clemens keeps asking me about going to Italy. I think it might eventually do her a great deal of good.

SAM

Well, when you're sure we can leave, I'll make arrangements.

DOCTOR

Very good.

He starts out.

SAM

(Rising)

Doctor …

DOCTOR

Yes?

SAM

(Crosses to him)

Is my wife going to get well?

DOCTOR

I have every hope, Mr. Clemens, and so must you.

He goes out of the room.

INT: LIVY'S SITTING ROOM—DAY.

Lettering on Screen: Florence, Italy—Spring 1904

LIVY *is lying propped up in bed. The nurse is by her bedside reading.* KATY *comes into the room.*

KATY

Good evening, Mrs. Clemens.

Taking coat off. NURSE *crosses to bureau.*

LIVY

Hello, Katy. Did you have a nice day?

KATY

Yes'm, but a tired one. I've walked all over the city of Florence.

Crosses. Sits by bed.

LIVY

Have you Katy? Well, I'm glad. I think it's one of the few days you have had to yourself in the year we have been here.

KATY

Oh, you've never seen anything like the sight I've seen. There were more great goings on at the Church and I went over to it. It's what they call "Forty Hours Adoration." It's a grand procession with boys carrying lighted candles and the priests going around to the different churches and then marching back to their own. I went around with them in that procession to all the different churches. I walked miles today.

LIVY

I bet you're tired.

KATY

How are you?

LIVY

I feel better.

NURSE

It's time for Mr. Clemens' visit. Shall I call him?

LIVY

Yes. If you will.

The NURSE *goes out.*

KATY

Let me fix this.

LIVY

Katy, Florence is resting me and wearing you out.

KATY

Oh, yes Ma'am. It is helping you, isn't it?

LIVY

I think so. In Riverdale we had the river and the snow and ice, and here, Katy, we've had the warm nights, and the smell of roses, and the scented laurel and orange blossoms. Any way in the night when I awake and I see you asleep over there, I can sometimes hear a nightingale sing sweetly, oh, so sweetly, but lonesome, too, and forlorn and one night I heard an owl and that frightened me because when I was a little girl I heard somewhere that owls were an omen of death.

KATY

Oh, no, no.

LIVY

But when I spoke to Mr. Clemens about it he told me that the priest next door told him they come back to this garden every year. They have a nest there and they visit it…

The **NURSE** *comes in.*

NURSE

Here's Mr. Clemens.

SAM *stands in the doorway.*

LIVY

Hello, Youth.

SAM

Hello, Livy.

NURSE

I'm going to rest, Katy, I'll leave her in your care.

KATY

All right.

The **NURSE** *goes out.*

LIVY

Katy, leave us alone for a little.

KATY

All right.

KATY *goes out.*

LIVY

Youth, come over to my bed.

SAM

I don't think I should, Livy. The nurse and the doctor have both cautioned me that only a word and a kiss are still permitted...

LIVY

It will do me no harm tonight. I feel so much stronger...

SAM

All right.

(He comes to her)

You do look stronger, Livy. I'm so glad we brought you here.

LIVY

I wish I could lie down flat again. It's been seven months since I've been flat... Open the window, Youth.

(He opens the window)

Smell the roses... Are the gardens beautiful?

SAM

Yes, they are.

(He comes over to her)

Before we left America I was going through some papers and I found this letter that I wrote you before we married and you must have saved it—I thought you might like to look at it sometimes.

LIVY

Thank you.

She takes it. He kisses her.

SAM

I'm going now… I don't want to tire you…

He goes to the door. She waves to him. He throws her a kiss. He goes out. LIVY *picks up the letter. She reads it to herself.*

LIVY

"…and to think that with all this exquisite loveliness should be joined such rare and beautiful qualities of mind and heart, is a thing that is utterly incomprehensible—Livy you are as kind and good and sweet and unselfish and just, and truthful, and sensible and intellectual as the homeliest woman I ever saw (for you know that these qualities belong peculiarly to homely women)."

(She puts the letter down for a moment while she catches her breath and then she takes the letter up again)

"I have so longed for these qualities in my wife, and have so grieved because she would have to be necessarily a marvel of ugliness—I who do so worship beauty. But with a good fortune which is a very miracle, I have secured all these things in my little wife to be—and beauty—beauty beyond any beauty that I ever saw in a face before. I…"

She lets the letter fall. KATY *comes into the room.*

KATY

(Crossing to window)

I just remembered about the windows. Who opened them?

LIVY

Mr. Clemens.

KATY

Do you want to sleep?

LIVY

I'll rest.

(**KATY** *starts out*)

But stay with me, Katy. Stay here with me…

(**KATY** *sits. We hear off* **SAM** *singing "Steal Away to Jesus."*)

He's playing the old songs. It's the first time I've heard him in so long—it's the first time he's sung them since Susy died.

She begins to gasp. **KATY** *goes to her. The* **NURSE** *comes into the room.*

KATY

You'd better get the oxygen. She's having trouble breathing again.

The **NURSE** *goes out of the room. The singing of* **SAM'S** *is now loud and clear and strong and vigorous.*

LIVY

Katy…Katy…help me! Help me!!

KATY

Nurse! Nurse! Hurry—Hurry—Mr. Clemens! Miss Clara! Miss Jean! Hurry! Hurry!

The **NURSE** *comes into the room. She goes to the other side of the bed and helps* **KATY** *hold her.* **CLARA** *and* **JEAN** *come into the room.*

CLARA

Katy, what is it?

CLARA *and* **JEAN** *see their mother and the terrifying struggle she is going through and they go in terror to the foot of her bed and stand, holding hands, watching.* **SAM** *comes into the room. He goes at once to his wife. He takes her hand. He kisses it.*

SAM

Livy…

He lets her hand go. They put her body back gently down on the bed. She is dead.

CLARA

Katy?

KATY *holds her and begins to cry.* **SAM** *puts his arms around his wife.*

SAM

How beautiful she is—how young and sweet—and look! She's smiling!

Then he lets her go and he is crying by the bed and **CLARA** *and* **JEAN**, *crying too.*

DISSOLVE TO: DECK OF BOAT.

SAM *is standing by rail.* **KATY** *comes up to him.*

KATY

How do you feel, Mr. Clemens?

SAM

Well enough. How are the girls?

KATY

They're in their cabins resting.

SAM

It was thirty-one years ago, Katy, Livy, and I made our first voyage together. Susy was a year old then. In my life, Katy, there have been sixty-eight Junes. How colorful sixty-seven of them are contrasted with the deep blackness of this one. Do you want to know something? I cannot reproduce Livy's face in my mind's eye. I was never in my life able to reproduce a face. It is a curious infirmity and now at least I realize that it is a calamity.

KATY

Where is the funeral to be, Mr. Clemens?

SAM

In Elmira. She'll be buried beside Susy and our boy. Do you know we had a son?

KATY

I remember Mrs. Clemens telling me, once.

SAM

He died when he was a baby. "In these thirty-four years," Katy, Livy and I have made many voyages together and now we are making our last—she down below and lonely; I above and lonely.

Mark Twain (played by Franchot Tone) gazes at the face of his daughter Jean (Jane McArthur), found dead in her morning bath on December 24, 1909. Katherine Squire, left, also appears in this production still from the closing stages of Horton Foote's *The Shape of the River*. Photograph courtesy CBS Photo Archive.

The Shape of the River opens in 1895 with a bankrupt Mark Twain (Franchot Tone) preparing for his round-the-world lecture tour. Making plans with him are, from left, daughters Clara (Nancy Rennick) and Susy (Shirley Knight), and his wife, Livy (Katharine Bard). Photograph courtesy CBS Photo Archive.

Videotaped at Television City in Hollywood, the *Playhouse 90* production of *The Shape of the River* used dozens of extras to depict several of Mark Twain's 1895 lectures. Photograph courtesy CBS Photo Archive.

Tone as Twain in his late sixties, wearing the white suit and puffing on the ever-present cigar. Photograph courtesy CBS Photo Archive.

Tone aged from fifty-nine to seventy-four in *The Shape of the River*, writer Horton Foote's *Playhouse 90* drama examining the last fifteen years of Mark Twain's life. Aired on May 2, 1960, the CBS presentation started in 1895 with Twain's battle back from bankruptcy and concluded shortly before his death in 1910. Photograph courtesy CBS Photo Archive.

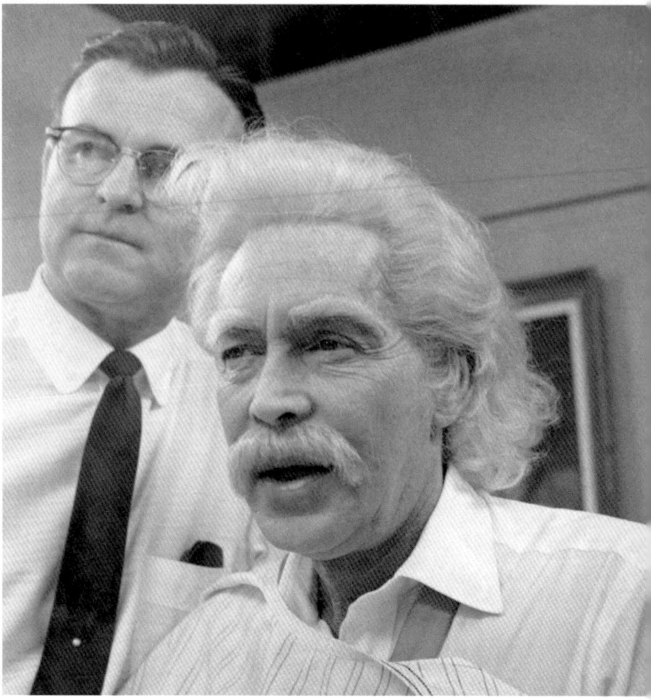

Fifty-five-year-old Franchot Tone spent about three hours in the makeup chair at the CBS Television City studios to play Mark Twain at sixty-seven and older in *The Shape of the River,* the next-to-last *Playhouse 90* drama. Photograph courtesy CBS Photo Archive.

Mark Twain explains how to reach old age in a scene depicting his seventieth birthday banquet at Delmonico's. Photograph courtesy CBS Photo Archive.

Franchot Tone was not the producers' first choice to portray Mark Twain in *The Shape of the River.* They were turned down by Fredric March, who had played the author of *Tom Sawyer* and *Huckleberry Finn* in *The Adventures of Mark Twain,* an entertaining but unreliable biography released by Warner Bros. in 1944.

Also offered the lead role in *The Shape of the River* was Hal Holbrook, the thirty-five-year-old actor who had captivated New York critics and audiences the year before with his one-man show, *Mark Twain Tonight!* Holbrook had been convincingly playing Twain at the age of seventy since 1954. Photograph courtesy of Hal Holbrook.

Franchot Tone won an Oscar nomination for his portrayal of Roger Byam, the midshipman who falls in love with a Tahitian named Tehani (Movita Castaneda) in *Mutiny on the Bounty* (1935).

Tone in the early 1950s, when his club-hopping ways often landed him in the gossip columns.

Tone as he appeared when *The Shape of the River* aired in 1960.

Five months after his appearance in *The Shape of the River*, Franchot Tone, left, visits Elmira College and is given a guided tour of Mark Twain's octagonal study by college president Dr. J. Ralph Murray. Photograph courtesy the Mark Twain Archive, Elmira College, Elmira NY.

Tone, carrying a wreath of fall leaves for Twain's headstone, admires the monument to the writer in Elmira's Woodlawn Cemetery. Photograph courtesy the Mark Twain Archive, Elmira College, Elmira NY.

Tone answers a newspaper reporter's questions over morning coffee at the Mark Twain Hotel in Elmira. Photograph courtesy the Mark Twain Archive, Elmira College, Elmira NY.

Shirley Knight, seen here in an early 1960s studio still, was twenty-two when chosen to play Susy Clemens.

John Frankenheimer, left, who was supposed to direct *The Shape of the River*, sits with Fred Coe, the TV pioneer who produced the *Playhouse 90* drama. Photograph courtesy of John Coe; NBC photo.

Horton Foote, a veteran of television's golden age of live drama, about the time *The Shape of the River* aired. Photograph courtesy of Horton Foote.

A recent picture of Horton Foote, whose honors include two Oscars, an Emmy, and the Pulitzer Prize. Photograph courtesy of Horton Foote.

Gregory Peck and Brock Peters starred in *To Kill a Mockingbird,* released two years after *The Shape of the River* aired on CBS. Horton Foote's screenplay adaptation of Harper Lee's novel won him the first of two Academy Awards. Peck's portrayal of lawyer Atticus Finch earned him the Oscar for best actor.

Foote's second Academy Award was for his original screenplay *Tender Mercies.* The 1983 film starred Robert Duvall (pictured here with Allan Hubbard), who, like Peck, won the Oscar for best actor.

During a July 1870 lobbying trip to Washington, a thirty-four-year-old Mark Twain stops at photographer Matthew Brady's studio to pose with his friend, poet-editor David Gray of the *Buffalo Courier*, and, at right, journalist George Alfred Townsend. Courtesy Library of Congress, Pictures & Prints Division

Mark Twain on board the U.S.S. Mohican in August 1895, launching the lecture tour depicted in *The Shape of the River*. Photograph courtesy the Mark Twain Archive, Elmira College, Elmira NY.

Twain, in Montana during the early stages of his 1895 lecture tour, poses at the Missoula station with Senator Wilbur F. Sanders. Photograph courtesy the Mark Twain Archive, Elmira College, Elmira NY.

Mark Twain, "almost an old man. . . patience torn to rags," struggling back from financial ruin, in 1895. It is at this dramatic point in his life that Horton Foote's *The Shape of the River* opens with Franchot Tone playing the writer at the age of fifty-nine. Photograph courtesy the Mark Twain Archive, Elmira College, Elmira NY.

"In the thick of the fight there is cheer," Twain said of his determination to pay his debts dollar for dollar.

During his last visit to Quarry Farm, Mark Twain again works in the cozy and isolated octagonal study built for him in 1874 by his sister-in-law, Susan Langdon Crane. Photograph courtesy the Mark Twain Archive, Elmira College, Elmira NY.

Mark Twain on the porch of Quarry Farm, Aunt Sue Crane's Elmira home where the Clemens family spent many cherished summers. Photograph courtesy the Mark Twain Archive, Elmira College, Elmira NY.

Mark Twain in his study on the Quarry Farm grounds during the 1903 trip to Elmira. Photograph courtesy the Mark Twain Archive, Elmira College, Elmira NY.

Also taken during the 1903 summer stay in Elmira, this picture shows Twain talking with free-born African American John T. Lewis, a family friend and tenant farmer on Susan Crane's upstate New York property. Twain used Lewis as one of the models for Jim in *Huckleberry Finn*. Courtesy Library of Congress, Pictures & Prints Division

Twain and Lewis at Quarry Farm in 1903. Twain was sixty-seven, about the age Franchot Tone played him during the second act of *The Shape of the River*, which starts in 1902 and concludes in 1904. Courtesy Library of Congress, Pictures & Prints Division

Mark Twain as many first think of him, with white hair and white suit (which he didn't begin wearing in public until 1906). Tone played Twain in his seventies for the last act of *The Shape of the River.* Courtesy Library of Congress, Pictures & Prints Division

Many actors followed Tone playing Twain on TV, including Jason Robards in the Disney Channel's *Mark Twain and Me.*

David Wayne appears as Sam Clemens in *The Adventures of Mark Twain,* an ABC special that aired on May 5, 1967.

Ken Howard, who played Twain on *Bonanza,* in the title role of *Pudd'nhead Wilson.*

Craig Wasson as Twain in the 1983 PBS version of *The Innocents Abroad.*

Jimmy Stewart portrays Twain for a special aired by ABC in 1978.

David Knell, right, plays cub pilot Sam Clemens to Robert Lansing's Horace Bixby in a 1980 version of *Life on the Mississippi.*

Royal Dano, right, plays Mark Twain to Ron Howard's Huckleberry Finn in a 1975 TV movie.

Christopher Stone, center, puts in a 1982 TV appearance as Mark Twain on an episode of *Father Murphy.*

A ninety-minute CBS presentation of Hal Holbrook's *Mark Twain Tonight!* became one of the TV events of 1967. Photograph courtesy of Hal Holbrook.

Act 3

INT: BEDROOM—HOTEL—DAY.

Lettering on Screen: New York City, 1905.
SAM CLEMENS, *in a full dress suit, is tying his tie. It's the evening of his seventieth birthday.* **JEAN** *and* **CLARA** *come into the room. They are in evening dress.*

CLARA

Papa, hurry. You're going to be late.

SAM

Is Howells here?

CLARA

Yes, he's waiting in the lobby.

He takes his coat and starts out of the room putting his coat on as he goes.

KATY

I know it's going to be a lovely evening, Mr. Clemens. I wish I could look in at you all.

JEAN & CLARA

Good night, Katy. We've got to hurry him along.

They go out into the hall. **KATY** *follows after them. She stands in the hall by the door to their suite watching them hurry down the hall to the elevator. A* **MAID** *turns the corner carrying linens. She stands by* **KATY** *watching the* **CLEMENS**.

MAID

Isn't that Mark Twain?

KATY

Yes. Colonel George Harvey is giving a dinner at Delmonico's Restaurant to celebrate his seventieth birthday.

MAID

Those his daughters with him?

KATY

Yes.

MAID

I read in the papers one of the girls has nervous trouble. Which is the one?

KATY

Miss Jean. The youngest...

MAID

And Clara's the one that's getting married?

KATY

Yes.

MAID

To a foreigner, isn't it?

KATY

Yes. To Mr. Gabrilowitsch. He's a very famous pianist, you know.

MAID

Do they live here at the hotel?

KATY

No. They live in the country.

*(*CLARA *comes hurrying back down the hall)*

What is it, Miss Clara?

CLARA

Father forgot his notes for his speech.

CLARA *runs past* KATY *and the* MAID *into the suite.* KATY *starts in after her.*

KATY

Can I help you?

CLARA

I have them.

She holds up some crumpled and disorderly looking papers as she hurries past KATY*, and back out into the hall.*

DISSOLVE TO: BANQUET.

Applause.

HOWELLS

(Standing)

Now, ladies and gentlemen, and Colonel Harvey, I will try to be greedy on your behalf in wishing the health of our honored and in view of his great age, our revered guest. I will not say, "Oh King, live forever! But oh King, live as long as you like!"

Applause. HOWELLS *sits.*

SAM

(Rising)

Thank you, Mr. Howells.... The seventieth birthday! It is the time of life when you arrive at a new and awful dignity. You can tell the world how you got there. It is what they all do. You shall never get tired of telling by what delicate arts and deep moralities you climbed up to that great place. You will explain the process and dwell on the particulars with senile rapture. I have achieved my seventy years in the usual way; by sticking strictly to a scheme of life which would kill anybody else.

(Laughs)

I will now teach. Since forty, I have been regular about going to bed and getting up—and that is one of the main things. I have made it a rule to go to bed when there wasn't anybody left to sit up with; and I have made it a rule to get up when I had to. It has saved me sound, but it would injure another person. I have made it a rule never to smoke more than one cigar at a time. I have no other restrictions as regards smoking. It has always been my rule never to smoke when asleep, and never to refrain when awake. It is a good rule. I mean, for me; but some of you know quite well that it wouldn't answer for everybody that's trying to get to be seventy. . .I have never taken any exercise, except sleeping and resting, and I never intend to take any. Exercise is loathsome. And it cannot be any benefit when you're tired; and I was always tired. But let another person try my way, and see whence he will come out.

INT: SAM'S BEDROOM—NIGHT.

SAM *is propped up in the massive Italian bed reading and writing, surrounded by papers. A cat is beside him.*

JEAN

Here's the mail Papa. There's a letter from Clara.

(She hands it to him. She fixes the bed.)

There's nothing else that you have to read. I can take care of the rest for you.

He is reading **CLARA'S** *letter.* **JEAN** *is going through the rest of the mail.*

SAM

Clara seems very happy in Switzerland.

JEAN

Yes, she does.

SAM

I don't believe she misses us at all.

JEAN

Father, a reporter called this morning and said his paper was carrying a story that your health was failing and that you were in critical condition ever since Clara's wedding. I think you should send in a denial.

SAM

What difference does it make?

JEAN

(Sitting by bed)

The Associated Press is carrying the story. It will be sent to Switzerland. Clara will see it and be very worried. You have to deny it for her sake.

SAM

All right.

(Hands her a pencil and paper)

To the Manager of the Associated Press, New York. "I hear the newspapers say I am dying. The charge is not true. I would not do such a thing at my time of life. I am behaving as good as I can. Merry Christmas to everybody—Mark Twain."

(**JEAN** *writes it down)*

Were you up early this morning?

JEAN

Six.

SAM

Did you have your cold bath?

JEAN

Yes. I haven't missed one all winter.

SAM

Katy thinks they're too strenuous, Jean.

JEAN

Father, I get in and then right out. I've never felt better in my life.

SAM

You've never looked better—but I don't want you doing too much. Paine is here now and he said last night he would like so much to take care of some of your duties.

JEAN

Oh, no, I don't need any help. Here's a letter from a woman who had heard your health is failing and she sent you an infallible remedy—shall I write her and thank her?

SAM

Yes, ma'am. You may say, "Dear Madam—I try every remedy sent to me. I am now on number sixty-seven. Yours is number two thousand six hundred fifty-three. I am looking forward to its beneficial results."

JEAN *writes it out.*

JEAN

Here's a letter from someone who wants to know if you have written anything after "Captain Stormfield's Visit to Heaven."

SAM

You may write and say I have written a great deal. I have

finished nothing. That nothing pleases me.

JEAN

He asks specifically what you are at work on now.

SAM

Say I am at present working with Mr. Albert Bigelow Paine on the biography he is writing, that I am also working on my autobiography in my own way and in my own time.

(He reaches over for some papers)

Don't write this down. I just want you to listen to it, Jean. In this autobiography I shall keep in mind the fact that I am speaking from the grave. I am literally speaking from the grave, because I shall be dead when the book issues from the press. I speak from the grave rather than with my living tongue for a good reason: I can speak thence freely.

(He puts the paper down)

I want to be minded in this, Jean. I don't want any of my autobiography to be published until after I'm dead. I have so instructed Mr. Paine and I want you and Clara to uphold him in it.

JEAN

All right, but what terrible things are to be in this book?

SAM

Nothing so terrible.

JEAN

But you sound so serious and solemn. I've never known you to sound so serious before.

SAM

Do I? Well, good. I'm not often allowed to be serious, I can tell you.

JEAN

Papa, I take you very seriously.

SAM

I know you do, Jean, and I thank you for it. I hope it's not too lonely for you here in the country?

JEAN

No, I love it here.

SAM

Have you finished all your Christmas shopping?

JEAN

Yes, and I have all my presents wrapped. Katy and I will decorate the tree tonight, and I'll label my packages.

SAM

You're not doing too much, are you?

JEAN

No.

(She rises and kisses him on the forehead)

Don't worry about me. You mustn't worry about me.

SAM

You're all I have to worry about with Clara married and gone so far away.

JEAN

Do you realize I haven't had a seizure in months?

SAM

I know. And to tell you the truth, I have never seen you looking so well. Just don't do too much, that's all. I want you to promise me that.

JEAN

I promise you.

There is a knock on the door.

SAM

Come in.

PAINE *comes in.*

PAINE

Good afternoon, Mr. Clemens. Jean.

JEAN

Is your room comfortable, Mr. Paine?

PAINE

Oh, very.

JEAN

What time will your family join us on Christmas day?

PAINE

Around nine.

JEAN

I'll phone this message to the papers, Father.

She goes out.

SAM

I've written out some more pages this morning. I've skipped around—I started today with my early life in Hannibal.

PAINE

What was that remark your brother made to you when you were working in his newspaper office?

SAM

He said my literature had attracted the town's attention, but not its admiration. I've included it somewhere in there.

PAINE

I tell you, Mr. Clemens, I'm having a little trouble in reconciling some of your dates and events.

(He hands him a piece of paper)

Now, I thought for sure you told me this happened before you were twelve and here you say you were fourteen. And over here is a man's name that was different than the one you mentioned before, nor did it happen exactly this way.

SAM

Didn't it? Well, I tell you when I was younger I could remember anything whether it happened or not; but I'm getting older and soon I shall remember only the things that never happened at all. Now you go on with your reading and don't worry about dates and things you've heard me say.

PAINE

Yes, sir.

SAM *hands more pages to* **PAINE**. **PAINE** *is reading them.*

INT: HALL—DAY.

A huge Christmas tree is there with many unopened presents piled underneath. **JEAN** *crosses in decorating the tree.* **KATY** *comes in, her arms piled high with presents.*

KATY

Some more presents just arrived, Miss Jean.

JEAN

Thank you, Katy. Just put them down there anywhere.

KATY

Your father asked me this morning how many you were sending out, and I said I didn't know exactly but I thought around fifty.

JEAN

Fifty-five.

KATY

Is that so? What did you get your father?

JEAN

Something he's always wanted. An enormous globe of the world.

KATY

Let me help you.

JEAN

All right, Katy. You take that side of the tree.

(In the distance we hear an orchestral playing some music)

That's father playing the orchestral—he's restless tonight. He wanted me to play billiards with him after supper, but I was too tired.

KATY

Where is Mr. Paine?

JEAN

In his room working, I believe.

MR. PAINE *comes into the hall.*

PAINE

Can I help you?

JEAN

No, Katy and I can do it all. We're not going to work much more tonight.

PAINE

Jean, I wish you'd let me take over some of your duties while I'm here.

JEAN

No, Mr. Paine. Father spoke to me about it this morning, and it really isn't necessary. I'm not working too hard and I promised Father I would take some time off in March and Katy and I would go with him to Bermuda. On Monday, I'm going to write reserving a house.

SAM *comes in.*

SAM

Oh, there you are, Mr. Paine. I stopped by your room to see if I could interest you in some billiards.

PAINE

You certainly can.

SAM

Come, massage my head, Katy. No one does it like you.

KATY

Yessir-

She goes and massages his head.

SAM

This afternoon I met a man up in the village and he said to me, "You know you wouldn't look so young if you had a bald head. How do you preserve that mop? How do you keep it from falling out?" Well, I said, as I always do, I think it remains with me because I keep it clean; by thoroughly scouring it with soap and water every morning, then rinsing it well, then lathering it heavily, and rubbing off the lather with a coarse towel, a process which leaves a slight coating of oil on each hair—oil derived from the soap. Now then we arrive at a curious thing. The answer to my explanation always brings about the same remark, that this gentleman gave forth, the root of it! This remark is never made in a doubtful tone, but in a decided one—as if the speaker has examined the matter and knows all about it. But when I ask, How do you know this? They never quite know how to answer, and neither did this fellow; and so, when I asked him if he has ruined his own hair by wetting it, it turns out that he doesn't wet it often lest he rot the roots of it. Therefore, he is not talking from his own experience; if I ask if he has personal knowledge of cases where the roots were rotted by wetting, it turns out that he hasn't a single case of this kind to offer; when I hunt him remorselessly home he has to confess at last that everybody says that water rots the roots of the hair.

*(*JEAN *and* KATY *continue decorating the tree)*

Goodnight, Jean.

JEAN

Kiss me on my cheek. I have a slight cold.

He kisses her on her cheek.

SAM

See she gets to bed soon, Katy.

KATY

I will. Good night.

PAINE

Good night.

JEAN

Good night, Mr. Paine.

KATY

Good night, Mr. Paine.

SAM *and* PAINE *leave.* KATY *and* JEAN *go back to work.*

JEAN

Katy, I'm taking my presents to the station early in the morning, so can I have my breakfast very early? I'd like my cold bath ready by seven.

KATY

All right. I'll tell Jennie to wake you and have your bath drawn. I'll see to your breakfast.

INT: JEAN'S BEDROOM—DAY.

JEAN *is fast asleep in bed.* JENNIE *comes into the room and gently shakes* JEAN.

JENNIE

Miss Jean. Miss Jean. It's seven. Your bath is driven.

JEAN

Thank you, Jennie. Is it a nice morning?

JENNIE

It's a lovely morning. Katy's getting your breakfast for you.

JEAN

Thank you.

She gets out of bed, puts on a wrapper, goes hurrying out of the room.

INT: KITCHEN—DAY.

KATY *is fixing breakfast.* JENNIE *comes hurrying in.*

JENNIE

Katy, you'd better come. Miss Jean has been in her bath half an hour. She usually just gets in and then right out again.

KATY

I'll go right away.

She hurries out, JENNIE *following after her.*

INT: HALL—DAY.

KATY *and* JENNIE *come running down the hall.* KATY *goes to the bathroom door. She knocks. She gets no answer and then opens the door and goes inside.* JEAN *is lying in the tub, her head resting against the side.* KATY *runs to her.*

KATY

Jennie. Come help me—Miss Jean is dead.

JENNIE *comes running into the bathroom.*

INT: SAM'S BEDROOM—DAY.

SAM *is standing by the window looking out. He hears a noise in the hall. He starts out of the room, when* KATY *comes in.*

KATY

Mr. Clemens, quick! Miss Jean is dead!

She goes running back out of the room. SAM *starts out of the room.*

INT: BATHROOM—DAY.

They enter.

KATY

Her heart must have suddenly gave way. I was in the kitchen when Jennie came for me.

He kneels down beside JEAN.

SAM

How beautiful she looks, Katy. How beautiful. She's happy now; she's with her mother and sister; and if I thought I could bring her back by just saying one word, I wouldn't say it.

He stays beside her.

INT: SAM'S BEDROOM—DAY.

SAM *seated at desk.* PAINE *enters.*

PAINE

I wish you'd try to get some rest. You have been up all night.

SAM

"I am setting it down. Everything. It is a relief to me to write it. It furnishes me an excuse for thinking."

(A pause)

I lost Susy thirteen years ago; I lost her mother…Jean lies yonder, I sit here, we are strangers under our own roof.… The snow is even heavier now—it's a pity Jean can't see the snow. I can't think—I can't remember what was her favorite music?

PAINE

I think she always liked Schubert's "Impromptu."

SAM

(Turning)

Will you play it on the orchestral when they get ready to leave with her, and add the "Intermezzo" for Susy, and the "Largo" for Mrs. Clemens.

(Turns)

When I hear the music I shall know they are starting. Tell them to set lanterns at the door, so I can look down and see them go.

PAINE

I will.

PAINE *goes out.* SAM *begins his writing again.* KATY *comes in.*

KATY

We'll be leaving for Elmira soon, Mr. Clemens. Are you sure you won't change your mind and come with us?

SAM

No, Katy. I can never see another person belonging to me laid into the grave.

(Schubert's "Impromptu" is heard on the orchestral)

You'd better go now, Katy. I think they're leaving.

KATY *goes on out.* **SAM** *gets up and goes to the window looking out. He goes back to his writing.*

EXT: YARD OF HOUSE—DAY.

We see **KATY** *and others getting into a carriage.*

INT: STUDY—DAY.

SAM *is seated by the window. The papers he had been writing are beside him on the table. There is a knock on the door.*

SAM

Come in.

PAINE *enters.*

PAINE

I thought I'd see if I could get anything for you.

SAM

Nothing, thank you.

(He hands the papers to **PAINE***)*

This is the last thing I'll ever write. It's about Jean's death. It can end my autobiography. It is the final chapter.

PAINE

You'll write again.

SAM

(Rising)

No. I've done with it. I came in with Halley's Comet in 1835; it's coming again this year, and I expect to go out with it.

PAINE

Well, why…

SAM

No. It will be the greatest disappointment of my life if I don't go out with Halley's Comet. The Almighty has said, no doubt. Now here are those unaccountable freaks; they came in together, they must go out together. Oh! I'm looking forward to that.

PAINE

Are you going to live on here now?

SAM

Yes, I intend to stay. The spirits of the dead hallow a house for me.

(Sits)

It was not so with the other members of my family. They could not bear it. Susy died in the house we built in Hartford. Mrs. Clemens would never enter it again. But it made the house dearer to me. I have entered it once since, when it was tenantless and silent and forlorn, but to me it was a holy place, and beautiful. It seemed to me that the spirits of the dead were all about me, and would speak to me, and welcome me if they could. I shall stay in this house. It's dearer to me tonight than ever it was before…

(Crosses to bed)

It's started snowing again. I would like it if you and your wife and children would come and live here with me, while we're working together.

PAINE

I know they'd be happy too.

SAM

It would be company for me.

PAINE *looks down at the paper in his hand.*

PAINE

I'll leave you alone now.

SAM

No, later. Talk to me awhile now.

PAINE

Which of your books is your favorite?

SAM

I don't know. Livy liked *Joan of Arc* best, and then *Prince and the Pauper.* Which do you like?

PAINE

Huckleberry Finn. You weren't Huck, were you?

SAM

No. I was Tom. I knew a Huck, though. I knew a Huck and an Injun Joe and a Muff Potter. But I was Tom. And my mother was Aunt Polly. Someone. Some critic remarked once that I had spent most of my latter professional life remembering the years, the world of my boyhood. I suppose they're right. I know more and more when I'm alone and I go back to the beginning, my beginning, remembering.

(**PAINE** *steals another glance at the manuscript.* **SAM** *sees him.)*

You can go now.

PAINE

Will you be all right?

SAM

Oh, yes—quite all right.

PAINE

(Rising)

I'll look in on you later.

SAM

Thank you.

PAINE *goes.*

SAM'S YOUNGER VOICE

"I was born the 30th of November, 1835, in the almost invisible Village of Florida, Monroe County, Missouri.... The Village contained a hundred people and I increased the population by one percent. It is more than many of the best men in history could have done for a town. It may not be the modest in me to refer to this but it is true. There is no record of a person doing as much—not even Shakespeare. But I did it for Florida, and it shows that I could have done it for any place—even London, I suppose."

*(**SAM** closes his eyes. Voice begins to read the opening chapter of* Tom Sawyer.*)*

"Tom."

(No answer)

"Tom."

(No answer)

"What's wrong with that boy, I wonder?"

"You, Tom?"

*No answer. **SAM** opens his eyes. He takes a puff on his cigar—he is smoking, thinking, remembering, crying.*

FADE OUT

Appendix A
Biographies

KATHARINE BARD (LIVY CLEMENS):
A Broadway veteran, Katharine Bard played Annie in the original 1939 production of *Life with Father*, starred in the 1943 wartime hit *Three's a Family*, and appeared with Alfred Lunt and Lynn Fontanne in the 1949–50 run of S. N. Behrman's *I Know My Love.* Moving into television in the early 1950s, she appeared in several *Studio One* dramas, three installments of *The Lux Video Theatre* and the *Westinghouse Studio One Summer Theatre* production of *Jane Eyre* (August 1952). She was in the original cast of Eddie Albert's 1952 CBS comedy, *Leave It to Larry*, but was quickly replaced along with four other regulars. Before being cast in *The Shape of the River*, she appeared in such *Playhouse 90* productions as William Gibson's *The Miracle Worker* (as Kate Keller in 1957) and Rod Serling's *The Velvet Alley*, which aired on January 22, 1959, and starred Art Carney and Jack Klugman. She also appeared in episodes of *Alfred Hitchcock Presents* (opposite James Best in "Death Sentence," which aired April 27, 1958), *Perry Mason* ("The Case of the Lost Last Act" in 1959), *The Alfred Hitchcock Hour* (*Columbo* creators Richard Levinson and William Link's "Day of Reckoning," which aired November 22, 1962), *Gunsmoke*, *The Rifleman*, *Sam Benedict*, *The Big Valley*, *The FBI*, and *CBS Playhouse* ("Secrets" in 1968). Her films include *The Interns* (1962), *Johnny Cool* (1963), *Inside Daisy Clover*

(1965), and *How to Save a Marriage (And Ruin Your Life)* (1968). She also appeared in a 1976 TV movie directed by Delbert Mann, *Francis Gary Powers: The True Story of the U-2 Spy Incident.*

JAMES BELL (JOHN BRIGGS):

Born December 1, 1891, James Bell appeared in dozens of films between 1930 and 1960. He had featured roles in two thrillers produced by Val Lewton, directed by Jacques Tourneur, and released by RKO in 1943—*I Walked with a Zombie* and *The Leopard Man.* His list of credits also includes several Westerns: *Streets of Laredo* (1949), *Buckaroo Sheriff of Texas* (1950), *Riding Shotgun* (1954), *A Lawless Street* (1955), *Tribute to a Bad Man* (1955), and *The Tin Star* (1957). Among his many other films are *I Am a Fugitive from a Chain Gang* (1932), *Private Detective 62 (Man Killer)* (1933), *Holiday Inn* (1942), *My Friend Flicka* (1943), *Thunderhead—Son of Flicka* (1945), *The Spiral Staircase* (1946), *Driftwood* (1947), *Dead Reckoning* (1947), *The Wrong Box* (1947), *The Millerson Case* (1947), *Black Eagle* (1948), *The Company She Keeps* (1950), *Arizona Manhunt* (1951), *Million Dollar Mermaid* (1952), *Japanese War Bride* (1952), *Crime Wave* (1954), *Black Tuesday* (1954), *Teenage Crime Wave* (1955), and Jack Webb's newspaper drama, *-30-* (1959). During his long Hollywood career, he played supporting roles in movies starring Paul Muni, William Powell, Edward G. Robinson, James Cagney, Humphrey Bogart, Bing Crosby, Fred Astaire, Randolph Scott, and Henry Fonda. In addition, his TV credits include four episodes of *Perry Mason.* He died October 26, 1973.

FRED COE (PRODUCER):

The prolific producer was born on December 23, 1914, in Alligator, Mississippi. He attended the Yale School of Drama for two years (1938–40) and began his broadcasting career in 1945 as production manager for NBC. After working with producer Worthington Miner on *Studio One*, Coe launched NBC's *Philco Television Playhouse* in 1948. Starting in 1951,

Philco began alternating with *Goodyear TV Playhouse.* Overseeing production on the two live anthology series, Coe recruited such young writers as J.P. Miller, Horton Foote, Gore Vidal, and Paddy Chayefsky. Having won an Emmy for best producer of a live series in 1955, Coe produced *Playwrights '56*, an NBC anthology that premiered in 1955 and was canceled the following spring. He rebounded in 1957 by moving to CBS and becoming one of the producers on *Playhouse 90.* After the golden age of live drama came to an end in the early 1960s, Coe continued to work in television, but on a less consistent basis. In 1976, he produced *The Adams Chronicles* for PBS and even directed several episodes. He also produced acclaimed film versions of works by writers from his golden-age shows: William Gibson's *The Miracle Worker*, Tad Mosel's *All the Way Home* (based on James Agee's *A Death in the Family*), and Herb Gardner's *A Thousand Clowns.* The man considered the foremost producer of live television dramas died in Los Angeles on April 29, 1979.

PHILIP COOLIDGE (ALBERT BIGELOW PAINE):
Born August 25, 1908, in Concord, Massachusetts, Philip Coolidge appeared with fellow *Shape of the River* cast member Leif Erickson in the 1939 Broadway run of *Margin for Error.* He also played Judge Hawthorne in the original 1953 production of Arthur Miller's *The Crucible*, and had a featured role in the 1957 Broadway production of Gore Vidal's *A Visit to a Small Planet.* He returned to Broadway in 1964 as Ambassador Voltemand in director John Gielgud's staging of *Hamlet* (starring Richard Burton). His notable film roles include con man Emmett Perkins in *I Want to Live!* (1958), theatre manager Ollie Higgins opposite Vincent Price in *The Tingler* (1959), Dr. Cross in director Alfred Hitchcock's *North By Northwest* (1959), Reverend Osgood in *The Mating Game* (1959), the mayor of Hillsboro in the film version of *Inherit the Wind* (1960), Mr. Porter in *The Russians Are Coming! The Russians Are Coming!* (1966), and Fingers Felton in *Never a Dull Moment*, a 1968 Disney comedy starring Dick Van Dyke. Between 1956

and 1959, he appeared in six episodes of *Alfred Hitchcock Presents*, including "The Perfect Murder" (1956) and "The Dusty Drawer," a 1959 episode co-starring Dick York (also in *Inherit the Wind*). His other television credits include episodes of *The Twilight Zone* ("A Piano in the House" in 1962), *Gunsmoke*, *Bewitched*, and *The Alfred Hitchcock Hour* ("Night of the Owl" in 1962). He also played butler Cooper Morley for a one-season stint (1963–64) on ABC's *The Farmer's Daughter.* He died of lung cancer on May 23, 1967.

LEIF ERICKSON (WILLIAM DEAN HOWELLS):

The tall, rugged actor was born William Wycliff Anderson on October 27, 1911, in Alameda, California. The son of a sea captain and writer, he was educated at UCLA. A former band vocalist and trombone player, he made his film debut as a soloist with the Ted Fio Rito Orchestra in *The Sweetheart of Sigma Chi* (1933). Switching to acting, he appeared in dozens of movies over the next forty-five years, including *College Holiday* (1936), *Conquest* (1937), *The Big Broadcast of 1938* (1938), *Ride a Crooked Mile* (1938), *Pardon My Sarong* (1942), *Arabian Nights* (1942), *Sorry Wrong Number* (1948), *The Snake Pit* (1948), *Show Boat* (1951), *Sailor Beware* (1952), *Abbott & Costello Meet Captain Kidd* (1952), *On the Waterfront* (1954), *Tea and Sympathy* (1956), *The Carpetbaggers* (1964), *Mirage* (1965), *Twilight's Last Gleaming* (1977), and *Hunter's Moon* (1979). He starred in "The Equalizer," a 1958 episode of *Alfred Hitchcock Presents*, and "The Monkey's Paw—A Retelling," a 1965 installment of *The Alfred Hitchcock Hour*, but his best-known television role was Big John Cannon in *The High Chaparral* (NBC, 1967–71). He served during World War II and was twice wounded in action. The first of his three wives was actress Frances Farmer. He died in 1986.

HORTON FOOTE (PLAYWRIGHT):

One of America's most prolific and honored writers, Horton Foote has won two Oscars, an Emmy, and the Pulitzer Prize for drama. Born in the small Gulf-coast Texas town of Wharton on March 14, 1916, Albert Horton Foote, Jr., started out to be an actor. He turned to writing in his early twenties as a member of the American Actors Theatre, which staged his one-act play, *Wharton Dance*, in the fall of 1940, and then his three-act work, *Texas Town*, the following spring. His first Broadway play, *Only the Heart*, appeared in 1944. In the 1950s, Foote became one of the leading contributors to television's golden age of live drama. His first teleplay for legendary producer Fred Coe was *The Trip to Bountiful*, which was broadcast in March 1953. It starred Lillian Gish, who reprised the role of elderly Carrie Watts for a Broadway production, while the 1985 film version won Geraldine Page an Academy Award for best actress. The ten plays Foote wrote for Coe in 1953 and 1954 included *A Young Lady of Property*, *The Midnight Caller*, and *The Oil Well.* His 1954 Broadway play, *The Traveling Lady*, vaulted Kim Stanley to stardom. It was turned into a 1965 film, *Baby, the Rain Must Fall*, starring Lee Remick and Steve McQueen. Foote's work for the landmark anthology series *Playhouse 90* included *Old Man* and *Tomorrow*, two adaptations of William Faulkner stories. *Tomorrow* was remade as a 1972 film starring Robert Duvall, and a 1997 *Hallmark Hall of Fame* version of *Old Man* won Foote an Emmy. His screenplay version of author Harper Lee's *To Kill a Mockingbird* (1962) brought him the first of two Academy Awards. The second was for an original screenplay, *Tender Mercies.* This 1983 film about a down-and-out country music singer also won Duvall an Oscar. In the early 1970s, Foote began writing a cycle of nine plays he called "The Orphan's Home." Several of these—*Convicts*, *Courtship*, *On Valentine's Day*, *1918*, and *Lily Dale*—have been produced as films. On cable, Foote has been represented by such works as *The Habitation of Dragons*, aired by Turner Network Television in 1992, and *Alone*, aired by Showtime in 1997. Produced by the Signature Theatre Company in New York City, Foote's *The Young Man from Atlanta* won the 1995 Pulitzer Prize for drama.

LARRY GATES (HENRY ROGERS):

Born September 24, 1915, Larry Gates got his start as an actor at the Barter Theatre in Abingdon, Virginia. First selected for the Barter by Laurette Taylor in 1939, Gates returned to the theatre many times (at one point in the same repertory company with Ernest Borgnine, Elizabeth Wilson, Herb Nelson, and Diane Cilento). His films include *Invasion of the Body Snatchers* (1956), *Cat on a Hot Tin Roof* (1958), *Some Came Running* (1958), *Toys in the Attic* (1963), *The Sand Pebbles* (1966), *In the Heat of the Night* (1967), *Hour of the Gun* (1967), *Airport* (1970), and *Funny Lady* (1975). On television, he appeared in episodes of *Alfred Hitchcock Presents* (including "Museum Piece" in 1961), *The Twilight Zone* (with fellow cast member from *The Shape of the River*, Sandy Kenyon, in "The Shelter"), *Route 66*, *Cimarron Strip*, *Then Came Bronson*, and *Lou Grant*. He portrayed Dean Rusk in the TV movie *The Missiles of October* and President Herbert Hoover in the miniseries *Backstairs at the White House*. For the last fifteen years of his life, he played H.B. Lewis on the daytime soap opera *Guiding Light*. He died of leukemia on December 12, 1996, in Sharon, Connecticut.

JERRY GOLDSMITH (COMPOSER):

One of Hollywood's most versatile and dependable composers, Jerry Goldsmith was born on February 10, 1929, in Los Angeles. After studying piano, composition, theory, and film scoring, he got his start in the early 1950s composing for radio programs. In the mid-1950s, he began working for various television shows. Over the next twenty years, he would compose scores for episodes of such shows as *Climax*, *Gunsmoke*, *Have Gun Will Travel*, *General Electric Theatre*, *The Twilight Zone*, *Thriller*, *The Man from U.N.C.L.E.*, *Police Story*, and *The Waltons*. The score for *The Shape of the River* was one of ten he composed for *Playhouse 90* productions (including Foote's adaptation of Faulkner's *Tomorrow*). His other TV work includes the scores for two acclaimed miniseries—*QB VII* (1974) and *Masada* (1981)—and the theme songs for *Dr. Kildare*, *The Man from U.N.C.L.E.*, *Room 222*, *Barnaby Jones*, *The Waltons*, and *Star Trek: The Next Generation*. He began composing for the big screen in 1957, and, at last count, had received thirteen Academy Award nominations. His many film scores include those for *Studs Lonigan* (1960), *Freud* (1962), *Lonely Are the Brave* (1962), *Lilies of the Field* (1964), *Seven Days in May* (1964), *Our Man Flint* (1966), *The Sand Pebbles* (1966), *Planet of the Apes* (1968), *The Illustrated Man* (1969), *Patton* (1970), *Papillon* (1973), *Chinatown* (1974), *The Wind and the Lion* (1975), *Logan's Run* (1976), *Magic* (1978), *Alien* (1979), *Star Trek: The Motion Picture* (1979), *Outland* (1981), *Poltergeist* (1982), *Gremlins* (1984), *Basic Instinct* (1992), *The River Wild* (1994), *Executive Decision* (1996), *Star Trek: First Contact* (1996), *Air Force One* (1997), *L.A. Confidential* (1997), *Mulan* (1998), *The Mummy* (1999), *Along Came a Spider* (2001), *The Sum of All Fears* (2002), and *Star Trek X: Nemesis* (2002). He won an Oscar in 1977 for *The Omen*. He won Emmys for the TV movie *The Red Pony* (1972), *QB VII* (1975), the TV movie *Babe* (1976), and *Masada* (1981).

SANDY KENYON (MAN AT HANNIBAL):

Born Sanford Klein on August 5, 1922, in New York City, Sandy Kenyon has been a familiar face in prime-time television since the early 1960s. He has been a regular on three network series, playing Shep Baggott on ABC's *The Travels of Jaimie McPheeters* (1963–64), Jim Lucas on the 1966–67 ABC comedy *Love on a Rooftop*, and Revered Kathrun on the 1984–85 season of the CBS evening soap *Knots Landing*. He has been a guest star or featured player in *Riverboat* (in 1960), three episodes of *The Twilight Zone* ("The Odyssey of Flight 33," "The Shelter," and "Valley of the Shadow"), five episodes of *The Dick Van Dyke Show* (playing a doctor and a police officer), *The Fugitive*, *Bonanza*, *That Girl*, *Gomer Pyle*, *The Partridge Family*, *All in the Family*, *Kung Fu*, *Barnaby Jones*, *Happy Days*, *Maude*, *Columbo*, *The Rockford Files*, *M*A*S*H*, *Lou Grant*, *The Bionic Woman*, *Hart to Hart*, *Crazy Like a Fox*, and *Designing Women*. He also appeared in director Boris

Sagal's 1974 TV movie *A Case of Rape* and such films as Elvis Presley's *Easy Come, Easy Go* (1967), *Tom Sawyer* (1973), Gregory Peck's *MacArthur* (1979), *When Time Ran Out* (1980), and *The Loch Ness Horror* (1982).

SHIRLY KNIGHT (SUSY CLEMENS):

The Emmy-winning actress was born Shirley Enola Knight on July 5, 1937, in Goessel, Kansas. She grew up in Lyons, Kansas, and attended Phillips University and Wichita University before studying theatre with Erwin Piscator and Lee Strasberg. She moved to Hollywood at the age of twenty, making her television debut the following year on NBC's *Matinee Theater*. Her stage career started with a role in a 1958 production of *Look Back in Anger* at the Pasadena Playhouse (where, coincidentally, Horton Foote had enjoyed an acting stint before turning his attention to writing). She made her film debut in *Five Gates to Hell* (1959), and received Oscar nominations for her work in director Delbert Mann's *The Dark at the Top of the Stairs* (1960) and Richard Brooks' *Sweet Bird of Youth* (1962). She made her New York stage debut in 1963. She has appeared in episodes of *The Outer Limits*, *The Fugitive*, *The Equalizer*, and *thirtysomething*. Her films include *The Group* (1966), *The Rain People* (1969), *As Good As It Gets* (1997), and *Divine Secrets of the Ya-Ya Sisterhood* (2002). She won a 1995 Emmy for her portrayal of Peggy Buckey in Home Box Office's *Indictment: The McMartin Trial*. She was nominated for a Tony in 1997 for *The Young Man from Atlanta*, the play that won her good friend Horton Foote the Pulitzer Prize.

LEN LESSER (PHOTOGRAPHER IN HANNIBAL):

The veteran character actor, best known for his many appearances as Uncle Leo on NBC's *Seinfeld*, was born in the Bronx on December 3, 1922. His many films include *Some Came Running* (1958, which also featured Larry Gates), *The Birdman of Alcatraz* (the 1962 movie directed by *Playhouse 90* graduate John Frankenheimer), *Kelly's Heroes* (1970), *Papillon* (1973), *The Outlaw—Josey Wales* (1976), and *House Calls* (1978). He also has appeared in episodes of *Everybody Loves Raymond*, *Mad About You*, *Boy Meets World*, *thirtysomething*, *Amazing Stories*, *Falcon Crest*, *Quincy*, *The Rockford Files*, *Kolchak: The Night Stalker*, *Kojak*, *Bonanza*, *All in the Family*, *Green Acres*, *That Girl*, *The Monkees*, *The Munsters*, *My Favorite Martian*, *Land of the Giants*, and *The Wild, Wild West*.

MOYNA MACGILL (NURSE):

Born in London on December 10, 1895, the English actress enjoyed a long career on stage, screen, and television. Known primarily as a theatre actress in Great Britain, she moved to the United States during World War II and started finding work in Hollywood, where her daughter, Angela Lansbury (born October 16, 1925), was making a name for herself with such films as *Gaslight* (1944) and *The Harvey Girls* (1946). She can be seen in three movies that feature her daughter: *National Velvet* (1944), *The Picture of Dorian Gray* (1945), and *Kind Lady* (1951). She had featured roles in *The Strange Case of Uncle Harry* (1945) and *Green Dolphin Street* (1947), and relatively small parts in *Forever and a Day* (1943), *Winged Victory* (1944), *The Uninvited* (1944), *Jane Eyre* (1944), *Frenchman's Creek* (1944), *The Clock* (1945), *Black Beauty* (1946), *Three Daring Daughters* (1948), *Texas, Brooklyn and Heaven* (1948), *Private Angelo* (1949), *Bride of the Gorilla* (1951), *Les Miserables* (1952), *The Unsinkable Molly Brown* (1964), and *My Fair Lady* (1964.) Both of her twin sons, Edgar and Bruce (born January 12, 1930), became producers. She died November 25, 1975.

JANE MCARTHUR (JEAN CLEMENS):

The year before *The Shape of the River* aired on CBS, Jane McArthur won the Drama Desk Award for her performance in a revival of Thornton Wilder's *Our Town*. The other Drama Desk winner for the 1958–59 season was Hal Holbrook for his New York production of *Mark Twain Tonight!* After *The Shape of the River*, McArthur stayed in the CBS family with a 1961–62 stint on the daytime soap opera *The Secret*

Storm. She also spent two years (1962–64) as Marion Gill on another CBS serial, *Search for Tomorrow.* In 1962, she played Jessica in the New York Shakespeare Festival production of *The Merchant of Venice.* The cast included George C. Scott as Shylock, Nan Martin as Portia, James Earl Jones as the Prince of Morocco, and William Devane as a servant to Bassanio. Produced and directed by Joseph Papp, the entire production was broadcast on New York's WCBS Channel 2 at 8:30 p.m. on June 21, 1962, from the Shakespeare Festival's new outdoor amphitheater in Central Park. It was the first broadcast of a complete play by Shakespeare from the theatre where it was being performed.

ELIZABETH PATERSON (WOMAN AT HANNIBAL):
Best known to generations of TV viewers as kindly neighbor Mrs. Trumbull on *I Love Lucy* (CBS, the 1953–56 seasons), the durable stage and screen actress was eighty-five when she played a Missouri woman hoping to get a glimpse of Mark Twain in *The Shape of the River.* She was born Mary Elizabeth Patterson on November 22, 1874, in Savannah, Tennessee. The daughter of a judge, she joined Chicago's Ben Greet Players in the 1890s (the decade in which the first act of *The Shape of the River* is set). Patterson specialized in Shakespearean roles until, in her forties, she started getting cast as devoted mothers, fussy aunts, gossipy matrons, high-society dames, and crotchety biddies. She made her Broadway debut in 1921, when Booth Tarkington personally chose her for his play *Intimate Strangers*, which starred Alfred Lunt, Billie Burke, and Frances Howard. With Broadway shows now regularly coming her way, she made her film debut in 1926. Perhaps her best-known screen performance was as Ada Lester in director John Ford's 1941 version of Erskine Caldwell's *Tobacco Road.* Her many other movies include *The Boy Friend* (1926), *The Return of Peter Grimm* (1926), *The Cat Creeps* (1930), *A Bill of Divorcement* (1932), *Dinner at Eight* (1933), *Bluebeard's Eighth Wife* (1938), *The Cat and the Canary* (1939), *Remember the Night* (1940), *Earthbound* (1940), *Belle Starr* (1941), *I*

Married a Witch (1942), *The Sky's the Limit* (1943), *Hail the Conquering Hero* (1944), *Colonel Effingham's Raid* (1945), *The Shocking Miss Pilgrim* (1947), *Welcome Stranger* (1947), *Intruder in the Dust* (1949), *Pal Joey* (1957), and *The Oregon Trail* (1959). She was in producer David O. Selznick's 1938 version of *The Adventures of Tom Sawyer*, and among her TV credits is a 1955 adaptation of Twain's *Adventures of Huckleberry Finn* for the CBS anthology series *Climax*. Her last movie, also made when she was eighty-five, was *Tall Story* (1960), which marked the film debut of Jane Fonda. She died on January 31, 1966.

NANCY RENNICK (CLARA CLEMENS):

Before being cast in *The Shape of the River*, Nancy Rennick played Patty Johnson, wife of rescue worker Skip Johnson (Lang Jeffries), on *Rescue 8*, the syndicated 1958–59 series based on the files of the Los Angeles County Fire Department's rescue squads. She also was a regular, playing social worker Edith Thorncroft, on *Kentucky Jones* (NBC, 1964–65), Dennis Weaver's post-*Gunsmoke* series about a veterinarian who adopts a Chinese orphan. In the same year as *The Shape of the River*, she appeared in an episode of *Chevy Mystery Theatre* ("I Know What I'd Have Done") and *The Twilight Zone* (Rod Serling's "The After Hours"). The following year, she appeared with fellow *Shape of the River* cast member Sandy Kenyon in another *Twilight Zone* tale, Serling's "The Odyssey of Flight 33." Her other TV credits include episodes of *The Outer Limits* ("The Hundred Days of the Dragon"), *Bonanza*, *Gunsmoke*, *Wagon Train*, *The Fugitive*, *My Favorite Martian*, and *The Farmer's Daughter*. She also appeared in the 1964 film *The Young Lovers*, which starred Peter Fonda.

BORIS SAGAL (DIRECTOR):

The prolific television director was born October 18, 1923, in Dnepropetrovsk, Russia. He studied at UCLA, Harvard Law School, and the Yale School of Drama. His many network credits include live television productions as well as episodes of *Alfred Hitchcock Presents*, *The Twilight Zone*, *Night Gallery*, *Columbo*, and *Amy Prentiss*. He also was at the helm of the miniseries *Masada* and such TV movies as *A Case of Rape* (1974), *The Greatest Gift* (1974), *The Runaway Barge* (1975), *The Oregon Trail* (1976), *Ike: The War Years* (1978), and *The Diary of Anne Frank* (1980). His big-screen films include *Twilight of Honor* (1963), *Girl Happy* (1965), *The Omega Man* (1971), and *Angela* (1977). He died on May 22, 1981.

KATHERINE SQUIRE (KATY LEARY):
Born March 9, 1903, the actress appeared with Kim Stanley in Horton Foote's *The Traveling Lady*, which opened on Broadway in October 1954. Her TV credits include three *Perry Mason* capers, two 1960 installments of *Alfred Hitchcock Presents* (Roald Dahl's "The Man from the South," with Steve McQueen betting Peter Lorre that his Zippo lighter will work ten times in a row, and "Pen Pal"), two trips to *The Twilight Zone* ("One More Pallbearer" in 1962 and "In His Image" in 1963), and an episode of *Dr. Kildare* (as the good doctor's mother). Her films include *The Story on Page One* (a 1959 movie written and directed by Clifford Odets and starring Rita Hayworth), *Studs Lonigan* (1960), *Days of Wine and Roses* (the 1962 version of the *Playhouse 90* drama), and *Ride in the Whirlwind* (an offbeat 1966 Western written and co-produced by its star, Jack Nicholson). She also appeared in *When Harry Met Sally*... (1989) in the "documentary" scenes, in which various couples talk about romance and relationships. She died March 29, 1995.

FRANCHOT TONE (SAM CLEMENS):
The son of a wealthy industrialist, Stanislas Pascal Franchot Tone was born on February 27, 1905, in Niagara Falls, New York. His childhood was one of privilege, which included the opportunity to travel around the world with his father, the president of the Carborundum Company. He attended

Cornell University, where he was president of the Dramatic Club. Although his father strongly disapproved, he decided on an acting career and made his professional stage debut with a Buffalo stock company in 1927. About a year later, he appeared on Broadway with Katharine Cornell in *The Age of Innocence.* The following season, he was back on Broadway in *Pagan Lady*, and in the early 1930s he was starring in *Green Grow the Lilacs* (the story turned into *Oklahoma!*). He also had one of the lead roles in the Group Theater's first presentation, *The House of Connelly*, which premiered on September 28, 1931. After appearing in the Group Theater's *Success Story*, Tone was offered a film role by MGM. There were other Broadway shows over the next twenty years (*A Thousand Summers* with Jane Cowl, *The Gentle People* with Sylvia Sidney, *The Fifth Column*, and *Hope for the Best*), but the actor spent most of these two decades in Hollywood, making about sixty movies. They included *Moulin Rouge* (1934), *The Lives of a Bengal Lancer* (1935), *Mutiny on the Bounty* (1935, for which he received an Oscar nomination for his portrayal of Roger Byam), *The Gorgeous Hussy* (1936), *Quality Street* (1937), *Three Comrades* (1938), *This Woman Is Mine* (1941), *Five Graves to Cairo* (1943), *Phantom Lady* (1944), *I Love Trouble* (1948), *Jigsaw* (1949), *The Man on the Eiffel Tower* (1950), and *Here Comes the Groom* (1951). In 1950, with his film career temporarily stalled, he turned to the fertile field of live television dramas, starring in productions for *The Philco Television Playhouse* ("Murder at the Stork Club" in 1950), *Tales of Tomorrow* ("The Horn" in 1952), *Suspense* ("All Hallow's Eve" in 1952), *Studio One* (one of the jurors in Reginald Rose's 1954 drama *12 Angry Men*), *Playwrights '56* (in a 1955 adaptation of Faulkner's *The Sound and the Fury*), *The Hallmark Hall of Fame* (Lillian Hellman's *The Little Foxes* in 1956), *The U.S. Steel Hour* ("Survival" in 1956), *General Electric Theater* ("Steinmetz" in 1956), *The Alcoa Hour* ("Night" in 1957), and *Westinghouse Desilu Playhouse* ("The Crazy Hunter" in 1958). He triumphantly returned to Broadway in the mid-1950s, starring in Eugene O'Neill's *A Moon for the Misbegotten* and Anton Chekhov's *Uncle Vanya.* His portrayal of Dr.

Mikhail Astroff earned him enthusiastic reviews and led to a 1958 film version of *Uncle Vanya.* For the next ten years, he moved from the stage to television to movies. He was in the 1962 film version of *Advise and Consent* (in which he played the president). Then there was the 1963 New York revival of O'Neill's *Strange Interlude.* He also had television appearances in *Alfred Hitchcock Presents* ("The Impossible Dream" with Mary Astor in 1959), *The Twilight Zone* (in Rod Serling's 1961 episode "The Silence"), *Wagon Train, The Virginian, Bonanza, The Alfred Hitchcock Hour* (Robert Bloch's "Final Performance"), and *Run for Your Life.* Additionally, he played Dr. Daniel Niles Freeland, the chief of surgery for the last season (1965–66) of ABC's *Ben Casey.* Married and divorced four times, each of his wives was an actress: Joan Crawford (1935–39), Jean Wallace (1941–48), Barbara Payton (1951–52), and Dolores Dorn-Heft (1956–59). He died September 18, 1968.

Appendix B
Mark Twain on Television
by Mark Dawidziak

I am grateful to Ken Burns, the late Howard Duff, James Garner, Hal Holbrook, Ken Howard, and the late Jason Robards for sharing their thoughts on Mark Twain and television.

—MARK DAWIDZIAK

Ken Burns peers into the clear afternoon sky, searching for an apt description of his latest PBS documentary. Sitting in a secluded corner of a plush Pasadena hotel's courtyard gardens, the effusive filmmaker has fallen uncharacteristically silent.

A moment before, the words were tumbling out at a furious pace. Now, he seems lost in reflection. Now, the only sounds filling the courtyard are the splashing of a nearby fountain and the distant drone of an airplane.

A smile returns to the still-boyish face warmed by the California sunshine. Somewhere in that remarkably blue sky, he has found his answer.

"I think," Burns says, speaking just above a whisper, "this is both the funniest and the saddest film we've ever made."

He's talking about *Mark Twain*, his four-hour biography of the writer who revolutionized American literature with such works as *Life on the Mississippi*, *The Adventures of Tom Sawyer*, *A Connecticut Yankee in King Arthur's Court*, and, of course, *Huckleberry Finn*.

The funniest? Well, that's certainly understandable. The writer born Samuel Langhorne Clemens in 1835 was a brilliant humorist, and this PBS documentary is loaded with hilarious examples of vintage Twain wit and wisecracks.

But the saddest, too? Burns is not succumbing to hyperbole here. Although the Emmy-winning filmmaker didn't realize it when he started planning the documentary, Mark Twain was all too familiar with tragedy.

As playwright Horton Foote discovered more than forty years earlier when researching *The Shape of the River,* his TV script about Mark Twain's last fifteen years, the writer's life was every bit as fascinating and dramatic as any of his stories.

Three of his four children died before him. He had to struggle back from a devastating economic collapse caused by poor business ventures. And he was crushed by the 1904 death of his beloved wife, Livy.

This is the writer Horton Foote hoped viewers would get to know when *Playhouse 90* aired *The Shape of the River* on May 2, 1960. This is also the writer Ken Burns showed America when his *Mark Twain* documentary premiered in January 2002.

"The overwhelming thing about this for me was finding out what an extraordinary writer he was," explains Burns, whose epic PBS documentaries have included *The Civil War*, *Baseball*, and *Jazz*. "He has no equal in American letters. That just stunned me. I read everything. I knew he was a great writer. I had no idea how great he was. We tend to take him for granted. And what's really incredible is how relevant his writing is today. There is so much of Twain that is a mirror of where we are today."

The subject of Burns' documentary would have liked that assessment. Mark Twain adored compliments almost as much as the cheap cigars he claimed were purchased at the bulk rate of four dollars a barrel ("but that includes the barrel"). Indeed, the writer estimated that he "could live for two months on a good compliment."

Based on the compliments bestowed on him by generations of writers, it's likely, then, that Twain's reputation as a literary giant will live for several centuries. To author and critic William Dean Howells, Mark Twain was nothing less than "the Lincoln of our literature," an assessment endorsed by Ernest Hemingway, Willa Cather, Robert Penn Warren, and Ralph Ellison.

Nobel Prize-winning writers, ranging from George Bernard Shaw to Toni Morrison, have sung his praises. And such comedians as Dick Gregory and Whoopi Goldberg have acknowledged his importance to their craft.

As novelist Russell Banks notes in the Burns documentary, we didn't really lose anything when Samuel Clemens died in 1910. That's because Mark Twain went on living through his books.

He also has gone on living through television, where he has been portrayed by dozens of actors since Franchot Tone played him in Foote's *The Shape of the River.* Before that *Playhouse 90* production, Twain's presence on television was mostly relegated to adaptations of his works. These include a musical version of *Huckleberry Finn* (starring Florence Henderson and Jimmy Boyd) on *The U.S. Steel Hour* and three live adaptations of *A Connecticut Yankee in King Arthur's Court* (including a 1952 *Studio One* version starring Thomas Mitchell and Boris Karloff). Though his works were well represented on the live-drama anthologies, Twain himself was rarely seen.

Perhaps the most prominent Twain-on-TV sighting before *The Shape of the River* was in one of the earliest episodes of NBC's long-running *Bonanza.* Aired in 1959, the Cartwright caper took advantage of the fact that the Ponderosa was near Virginia City and that Mark Twain got his start on that wide-open town's *Territorial Enterprise* newspaper in 1862 (a period described in his 1872 book, *Roughing It*).

This gave the episode a lot more historical grounding than a later *Bonanza* story that had Charles Dickens (played by Jonathan Harris of *Lost in Space* fame) visiting the Nevada Territory, presumably on his 1867–68 American tour. Dickens gave seventy-six readings during that visit, but he never made it west of the Mississippi. Getting him all the way to the Ponderosa was a bit of a stretch.

Still, the 1959 Mark Twain episode hardly is a model of historical accuracy. Let's just say that the reports of his Virginia City adventures are greatly exaggerated. Howard Duff, then best known for playing mystery writer Dashiell Hammett's hardboiled detective hero on radio's *The Adventures of Sam Spade*, was cast as Sam Clemens, who first riles then charms the Cartwrights.

"I had played Sam Spade as a little bit of a smart ass," Duff said, "and Sam Clemens starts out as a little bit of a smart ass in that episode. I don't know, I guess he was. But this was the young Mark Twain, so I wasn't going to do Hal Holbrook in the white suit and the white hair. This was Mark Twain at the very beginning of his career."

It was also *Bonanza* at the beginning of its TV career. The Twain encounter was the show's fifth episode. Then, about thirteen years later, the Western revisited the Ponderosa. Ken Howard, at the time best known for playing Thomas Jefferson in the Broadway musical *1776*, was chosen to play Sam Clemens in a story as fanciful as the one that featured Duff.

"It was 1972 and it was my first job in television," recalls Howard, who later had the title role in *The White Shadow*. "It also was the first episode of *Bonanza* after the death of Dan Blocker. Leo Penn directed it, and he took me to his house once, and there was his son, little Sean Penn, running around. I played Samuel Clemens with the mustache, but, of course, I'm so tall and Twain wasn't a particularly tall individual. They couldn't have me dwarfing Lorne Greene, so, if you'll notice in that episode, I'm always sitting down, spewing out all this stuff. Hal Holbrook, it isn't. But it was a fun shoot, and at the end of it, Michael Landon got up to talk and just broke down. He said, 'It's just not the same, and we all know it.' It was so moving. He just missed Blocker so much."

Fifteen years later, Howard was in London for a production of Eugene O'Neill's *Strange Interlude*. His co-star, Glenda Jackson, was amused when she caught a rerun of the American series on British television. "Last night," she informed Howard, "I saw you playing Samuel Clemens in *Bonanza*, of all things." Howard asked her how she liked it. "Well," Jackson replied carefully, "it was all right."

Bonanza ended its fourteen-season NBC run in January 1973, so Mark Twain appeared in one of the Western's very first and very last episodes. But Howard's association with the writer did not end with his trip to the Ponderosa. In 1984, he had the title role in an adaptation of *Pudd'nhead Wilson*, which aired on the PBS series *American Playhouse.*

By then, Twain sightings on television had become common. Shortly after *The Shape of the River*, Andrew Prine appeared as young Sam Clemens and James Daly as the older Mark Twain in an NBC presentation of *Roughing It*, which aired in May 1960. David Wayne played the writer in *The Adventures of Mark Twain*, an ABC special that aired on May 5, 1967. In 1975, Royal Dano appeared as Twain in segments filmed for the TV movie take on *Huckleberry Finn* (with Ron Howard as Huck, Donny Most as Tom, and Antonio Fargas as Jim). Five years later, David Knell played young Sam Clemens to Robert Lansing's Horace Bixby in a 1980 PBS adaptation of *Life on the Mississippi.* Gary McCleery played the character based on Sam in a 1981 PBS dramatization of the story "The Private History of a Campaign that Failed." In a 1982 episode of NBC's *Father Murphy*, Christopher Stone played another young Sam. Craig Wasson played Twain in a 1983 PBS version of *The Innocents Abroad* (in the middle of a seven-year flurry of public-television Twain programs that started in 1979 with "The Man that Corrupted Hadleyburg" and culminated in 1986 with an ambitious miniseries rendering of *Huckleberry Finn).* And even Jimmy Stewart donned Twain's white suit in 1978 for the ABC special "The General Electric All-Star Anniversary," which aired on September 29. In addition to Stewart, the celebrity lineup of that special included Henry Fonda, Lucille Ball, John Wayne, Red Skelton, Michael Landon, and Cheryl Ladd.

Yet by far the most important Mark Twain program that aired between Horton Foote's *The Shape of the River* and the Burns documentary *Mark Twain* was the CBS ninety-minute presentation of Hal Holbrook's *Mark Twain Tonight!* on March 6, 1967.

Holbrook had been bringing Twain to life for twenty years. As such, the two had been regular traveling companions, taking many roads to arrive at this electrifying moment in television history. An estimated 30 million viewers tuned in to see this remarkable program.

The Cleveland native was a mere twenty-two when he first stepped into Twain's white suit at a 1947 show staged in the suicide ward of the Chillicothe Veterans' Hospital in Ohio. The actor was a smooth-featured twenty-nine when he started regular tours of *Mark Twain Tonight!*—playing the seventy-year-old Twain in nightclubs and at schools. He was thirty-four when his one-man show became one of the most celebrated events of the 1959 New York theatre season (prompting Coe and Foote to offer him *The Shape of the River*). He was forty-one when his 1966 Broadway revival won him a Tony award. And he was forty-two when CBS aired its version, so well-remembered by so many.

Mark Twain once observed that there was "no surer way to find out whether you like people or hate them than to travel with them." Hal Holbrook certainly has had ample opportunity to put this maxim to the maximum test. He and Twain have been constant traveling companions for about fifty years. The long and winding road also can be measured in terms of performances—about 2,000.

"The truth is that he's been wonderful company," Holbrook says. "He's funny. He's incredibly insightful. He's a profound thinker. And almost every thought he uttered for public consumption in the last century has relevance today. What more could you ask for? It would be an understatement to say I like him. He never ceases to amaze me. Even after all these years, I'm still stunned by his insight into the human character. So much of what he had to say more than 100 years ago is right on the money for today. I can't get over this man. He just keeps coming."

Upon landing such a show in Manhattan, many actors would have figured, "Well, now I've made it. I've got my two hours of material, and I can live off these two hours for the rest of my life." Holbrook had the opposite reaction: "I've always been filled with fear, ever since the New

York critics bowed down and put a nice carpet under my feet in 1959. I was frightened to death that this show would kill me off as an actor. I was desperate not to let that happen. I was determined not to grow complacent or comfortable. One of the ways I fought that off was to pursue as many different kinds of projects as possible. The other was to keep adding material to the Twain show. And it's still growing. It's still a work in progress."

So the actor is constantly reshaping and reevaluating his landmark show to make sure it reflects the times. He has "gone through" at least fifteen hours of Twain material, adding new passages when they seem particularly relevant.

"He's a magnificent mouthpiece," says Holbrook, who schedules about forty *Mark Twain Tonight!* appearances each year. "At the height of the civil rights movement, I could take Twain into the Deep South and indict racism, prejudice, and bigotry. *I* couldn't have gotten away with saying those things. But they took Twain to their heart, and they listened to him."

Produced by David Susskind, the 1967 television version of *Mark Twain Tonight!* (released on video by Kultur in 1999) allowed Holbrook to voice not only Twain's views on prejudice, but also his anti-war sentiments.

"You know, I think I would end up in a mental institution if I couldn't do this Mark Twain show," he says. "I get so angry about what's going on in the world, I can barely contain myself. And this show gives you the freedom to go out on stage and say exactly what you're feeling—exactly what needs to be said. It's tremendously cathartic."

He also gets "pretty worked up" when *Huckleberry Finn* is attacked as a racist book.

"We will always be discussing these issues because we're still fighting the fight against racism in this country," Holbrook says. "It's a discussion that needs to be advanced. But *Huckleberry Finn* is a book about racism. It is not a racist book. I don't think anyone has put this into better perspective than (Nobel Prize-winning author) Toni Morrison in her wonderful introduction to the Oxford edition of *Huckleberry Finn*."

In her essay, Morrison calls attempts to ban *Huckleberry Finn* an "elementary kind of censorship designed to appease adults rather than educate children.... What (*Huckleberry Finn*) cannot be is dismissed. It is classic literature, which is to say it heaves, manifests, and lasts."

Holbrook agrees with Morrison that *Huckleberry Finn*, far from being a racist book, is an attack on a racist society and racist attitudes, and so he includes long passages from the novel in his 1967 telecast. He also refused to remove the N-word that made such a stir at the O.J. Simpson trial.

"And, yes, he uses satire and exaggeration to make his point," Holbrook says, "but that's part of the genius of the book. It is sometimes painful to read, but that's because Twain is pushing our nose into painful realities. The material and the audiences rise above the political correctness issue. Look, frightened and faint-hearted people don't know how to think. They're absolutely paralyzed by political correctness. They're so frightened of a word, they miss the larger issue. They miss the wonderful message that preaches against prejudice and hatred. We get so distracted by these truly small-minded deviations like political correctness, that we don't deal with the big problems that are becoming almost insurmountable in our society."

The actor still spends about two hours with his makeup box to look old enough to convincingly play Twain at seventy. Ironically, Holbrook turned seventy in 1995.

For many, Holbrook has become the "voice" of Mark Twain. The tape of the 1967 broadcast explains why. Fully conscious of the power of what Twain called "a rightly timed pause," Holbrook again and again lures the audience in with his sublime delivery. Once he has us set up, he snaps the surprise punch line, tossing it off as if it were an afterthought and, as Twain advised, doing "his best to conceal the fact that he even dimly suspects that there" was anything funny about it.

The first act goes for the big laughs, starting with Twain's thoughts on railroad travel and smoking, moving swiftly to Holbrook's masterful rendition of "His Grandfather's Old Ram." This is Twain as the foremost standup comedian of his day.

The second act takes on a less light-hearted tone, with its caustic comments on slavery, its discussion of man as "the Creator's pet," and a generous sampling from *Huckleberry Finn* (including Pap Finn's rant against the government and Huck's battle with his conscience). This is Twain the social critic, attacking hypocrisy and ignorance.

The third act starts with a telling of the "Golden Arm" ghost story, cruises through an excerpt from *Life on the Mississippi*, and concludes with the moving "Mary Ann" farewell (adapted from a passage in Richard Henry Dana's *Two Years Before the Mast*). This is the philosophical Twain, contemplating the fragility of youthful dreams.

After *The Shape of the River*, television also continued to turn to Twain's writings as a source for TV movies and series. Disney aired a new version of *The Prince and the Pauper* in 1962 (with Sean Scully in a dual role and Guy "Zorro" Williams as Miles Hendon). There was *The New Adventures of Huck Finn*, a short-lived 1968–69 children's series on NBC. And within weeks of the big-screen musical version of *Tom Sawyer* hitting theatres in 1973, CBS aired its own adaptation as a TV movie. The cast included Josh Albee as Tom, Buddy Ebsen as Muff Potter, Jane Wyatt as Aunt Polly, and Vic Morrow as Injun Joe.

There was *Rascals and Robbers—The Secret Adventures of Tom Sawyer and Huckleberry Finn*, a CBS movie that aired in 1981. The PBS Twain programs included "The War Prayer" in 1981 and "The Mysterious Stranger" in 1982. There was also *Sawyer and Finn*, a 1983 pilot for a proposed series about Tom and Huck as adults. In 1985, Drew Barrymore and Brandy Ward starred in *The Adventures of Con Sawyer and Hucklemary Finn* an ABC modern-day gender twist. NBC aired a 1989 version of *A Connecticut Yankee in King Arthur's Court* starring Keshia Knight Pulliam of *The Cosby Show*. Also in 1989 was the *American Playhouse* presentation of David Birney's *The Diaries of Adam and Eve*.

Cable television networks also aired programs based on Twain's works. Home Box Office created an animated *Tom Sawyer* series in the late 1980s. The Disney Channel aired *Back to Hannibal: The Return of Tom Sawyer and Huckleberry Finn*, which also embraced the idea of Tom and Huck as adults (missing the fact that St. Petersburg is the name Twain gave Tom and Huck's boyhood home). In 1998, Disney created *A Knight in Camelot*, another twist on *Connecticut Yankee*, starring Whoopi Goldberg and airing on ABC.

This all reflected what was happening in the film industry. During this same period, there were new film versions of *Tom Sawyer*, *Huckleberry Finn*, *The Prince and the Pauper*, and *A Connecticut Yankee in King Arthur's Court*. However, television, as already mentioned, explored two areas untouched by the movies: documentaries and dramas about Mark Twain.

Two notable TV productions presented different takes on the period of Mark Twain's life covered in *The Shape of the River.* The first was *Mark Twain: Beneath the Laughter*, a sixty-minute program that PBS premiered on December 15, 1979. Irish actor Dan O'Herlihy played Twain, who, when the story begins, is returning from Bermuda in late 1909 with biographer Albert Bigelow Paine (Lyn Seibel).

Like *The Shape of the River*, *Beneath the Laughter* depicts the death of Jean Clemens on December 24, 1909, and shows Twain writing the essay known as "The Death of Jean." Unlike *The Shape of the River*, the script by Gill Dennis and Larry Yust brings to life scenes from Twain's books as the writer reflects on his past.

It was followed by *Mark Twain and Me*, a cable movie that the Disney Channel premiered on December 1, 1991. Two-time Oscar winner Jason Robards played Twain in the story loosely based on the author's friendship with a young fan named Dorothy Quick (Amy Stewart). Talia Shire (from *Rocky* and the *Godfather* trilogy) portrayed Jean and R.H. Thomson was cast as Paine.

Often charming and frequently inaccurate, *Mark Twain and Me* takes several actual incidents from Twain's life and wraps them around the friendship with young Dorothy (whose memories of these years were published in her 1961 book, *Enchantment*). Still, the script by Cynthia Whitcomb almost takes as many liberties as, say, *The Adventures of Mark Twain*, the highly unreliable 1944 film biography starring Fredric March.

"It's a very simple little story," said Robards, who won back-to-back Academy Awards for playing Ben Bradlee in *All the President's Men* (1976) and Dashiell Hammett in *Julia* (1977). "I was afraid at first that it might be too sweet, but the director, Dan Petrie, convinced me to do it, and I'm glad he did. I thought it turned out very well, but I did have a moment where I thought, 'Now, wait, is this stepping on what Hal Holbrook does? I love Hal, and I hope he's not mad at me for doing this.' "

Quite the contrary, for Holbrook had made it a practice to turn down such projects because they would, by necessity, take liberties with Twain's words and life.

Robards had first seen Holbrook perform *Mark Twain Tonight!* in 1959. They both had played Lincoln in TV dramas (Holbrook winning one of his five Emmys for *Sandburg's Lincoln*), and Holbrook also was in *All the President's Men* (as Deep Throat) and *Julia*.

"I'm glad Hal has that rule," Robards said. "He's made a lot of work for the rest of us. But his fingerprints must be on every one of these scripts. We'd all have to step aside if he wanted to do them. He's a remarkable actor."

Robards was no stranger to playing real-life people. In addition to Bradlee and Hammett, he had portrayed Abraham Lincoln, Ulysses S. Grant, Howard Hughes, Doc Holliday, and Andrei Sakharov. He won an Emmy for playing Henry Drummond, the character based on lawyer Clarence Darrow, in a 1980s remake of *Inherit the Wind*.

"I hadn't read much Mark Twain as a kid," he said. "I appreciated him more when I was older and am encouraging my kids to read him. And the more you dig, the more you discover."

Another popular Emmy-winning actor would don Twain's white suit for *Roughing It*, a two-part cable adaptation premiered by the Hallmark Channel in March 2002. James Garner, who played Wyatt Earp to Robards' Doc Holliday in *The Hour of the Gun* (1967), portrayed Twain for the four-hour production.

Like the 1960 NBC version, the Hallmark dramatization featured a young Sam Clemens (played by Robin Dunne) and an older Mark Twain (Garner). The two-parter opened with a white-haired Twain dressed in a white suit delivering the commencement address at his daughter Susy's graduation from Bryn Mawr.

For Twain experts, it was a game of spot the errors. Twain's hair had not yet turned white in the early 1890s. He hadn't started wearing white suits in public. And Susy only attended Bryn Mawr for a year.

Garner's affection for Twain, however, was genuine: "I love Mark Twain. I think he's our great American writer. I think he's at the top of the heap. But more than just a great writer, he's a tremendously interesting man. And *Roughing It* is this tremendous story about people going out to hunt for gold and to strike it rich. And most didn't do it, including him."

Well, he actually did find gold in the Nevada Territory, but not at the end of a miner's shovel. He found it at the end of a reporter's pen.

Garner also rode to fame in the late 1950s as Bret Maverick, a different kind of cowboy hero. Sly, sarcastic, and wonderfully opportunistic, this "legend of the West" was just the type of roguish character Mark Twain would have loved. So perhaps it wasn't that big a leap from Bret's familiar black outfit to Twain's trademark white suit.

Television documentaries about Mark Twain include one narrated by Mike Wallace for the syndicated *Biography* series (1961–64), another for Greystone Communications' 1995 installment of A&E's cable series of biographies, the Learning Channel's *Great Books* episode on *Huckleberry Finn*, PBS's 1999 presentation of the four-part travelogue *On the Trail of Mark Twain with Peter Ustinov*, and the January 2000 PBS show

Born to Trouble: Adventures of Huckleberry Finn. Then, in 2002, there was Ken Burns, fascinated by the aspects of Twain's life that so intrigued Horton Foote. Burns' *Mark Twain* documentary features interviews with leading Twain scholars and such authors as Arthur Miller, William Styron, and David Bradley. Yet Burns decided to keep the "talking heads" to a minimum this time around, wisely letting Twain do most of the talking (through actor Kevin Conway).

"You can't do better than Twain," says Burns, who worked with a script by Dayton Duncan and Geoffrey C. Ward. "The smartest thing you can do is get out of his way and let him tell the story."

He counts himself lucky to have found three "wonderfully eloquent voices" to narrate the four-hour biography. The first belongs to novelist Russell Banks; the second belongs to Pulitzer Prize-winning journalist Ron Powers, who grew up in Hannibal; and the last belongs to Hal Holbrook.

"Russell Banks says that the two great American themes are race and space," Burns notes. "In Mark Twain, we have someone who can look those twin issues square in the face and write beautifully. What is more incredible than that? In Twain's example, we find inspiration, brotherhood, and enormous sympathy... The great thing about Twain was that he acknowledged the contradictions in himself. He said that the human race was a parade of fools, and he was not only marching in that parade, he was carrying a banner. He said, 'I am only human, although I regret it.' He said that he was the entire human race, frailties and all, compacted into a single suit of clothes. And I think he was right."

Appendix C "The Death of Jean" by Mark Twain

When his youngest daughter, Jean, died on the morning of December 24, 1909, a grief-stricken Mark Twain almost immediately felt compelled to put his feelings down on paper. Working for two days, he completed the 4,300-word essay that Twain scholar R. Kent Rasmussen calls "the last substantial writing he ever completed." The piece was first published in *Harper's Magazine* about eight months after Mark Twain's death on April 21, 1910. It then appeared in the 1917 collection *What Is Man? and Other Essays*, the 1959 version of *The Autobiography of Mark Twain* (edited by Charles Neider), and *Mark Twain's Own Autobiography* (1990, edited by Michael J. Kiskis).

Horton Foote used the incredibly poignant essay when writing *The Shape of the River*, and many details from "The Death of Jean" can be found in the *Playhouse 90* production.

"The Death of Jean"

(as it appears in *What Is Man? and Other Essays*)

The death of Jean Clemens occurred early in the morning of December 24, 1909. Mr. Clemens was in great stress of mind when I first saw him, but a few hours later I found him writing steadily.

"I am setting it down," he said, "everything. It is a relief to me to write it. It furnishes me an excuse for thinking." At intervals during that day and the next I looked in, and usually found him writing. Then on the evening of the 26th, when he knew that Jean had been laid to rest in Elmira, he came to my room with the manuscript in his hand.

"I have finished it," he said; "read it. I can form no opinion of it myself. If you think it worthy, some day—at the proper time—it can end my autobiography. It is the final chapter."

Four months later—almost to the day—(April 21st) he was with Jean.

—**ALBERT BIGELOW PAINE.**

Stormfield, Christmas Eve, 11 A.M., 1909.

JEAN is dead!

Has any one ever tried to put upon paper all the little happenings connected with a dear one—happenings of the twenty-four hours preceding the sudden and unexpected death of that dear one? Would a book contain them? Would two books contain them? I think not. They pour into the mind in a flood. They are little things that have been always happening every day, and were always so unimportant and easily forgettable before—but now! Now, how different! how precious they are, now dear, how unforgettable, how pathetic, how sacred, how clothed with dignity!

Last night Jean, all flushed with splendid health, and I the same, from the wholesome effects of my Bermuda holiday, strolled hand in hand from the dinner-table and sat down in the library and chatted, and planned, and discussed, cheerily and happily (and how unsuspectingly!)—until nine—which is late for us—then went upstairs, Jean's friendly German dog following. At my door Jean said, "I can't kiss you good night, father: I have a cold, and you could catch it." I bent and kissed her hand. She was moved—I saw it in her eyes—and she impulsively kissed my hand in return. Then with the usual gay "Sleep well, dear!" from both, we parted.

At half past seven this morning I woke, and heard voices outside my door. I said to myself, "Jean is starting on her usual horseback flight to the station for the mail." Then Katy [fn. 1: Katy Leary, who had been in the service of the Clemens family for twenty-nine years.] entered, stood quaking and gasping at my bedside a moment, then found her tongue:

"Miss Jean is dead!"

Possibly I know now what the soldier feels when a bullet crashes through his heart.

In her bathroom there she lay, the fair young creature, stretched upon the floor and covered with a sheet. And looking so placid, so natural, and as if asleep. We knew what had happened. She was an epileptic: she had been seized with a convulsion and heart failure in her bath. The doctor had to come several miles. His efforts, like our previous ones, failed to bring her back to life.

It is noon, now. How lovable she looks, how sweet and how tranquil! It is a noble face, and full of dignity; and that was a good heart that lies there so still.

In England, thirteen years ago, my wife and I were stabbed to the heart with a cablegram which said, "Susy was mercifully released today." I had to send a like shot to Clara, in Berlin, this morning. With the peremptory addition, "You must not come home." Clara and her husband sailed from here on the 11th of this month. How will Clara bear it? Jean, from her babyhood, was a worshiper of Clara.

Four days ago I came back from a month's holiday in Bermuda in perfected health; but by some accident the reporters failed to perceive this. Day before yesterday, letters and telegrams began to arrive from friends and strangers which indicated that I was supposed to be dangerously ill. Yesterday Jean begged me to explain my case through the Associated Press. I said it was not important enough; but she was distressed and said I must think of Clara. Clara would see the report in the German papers, and as she had been nursing her husband day and night for four months [fn. 2: Mr. Gabrilowitsch had been operated on for appendicitis.] and was worn out and feeble, the shock might be disastrous. There was reason in that; so I sent a humorous paragraph by telephone to the Associated Press denying the "charge" that I was "dying," and saying "I would not do such a thing at my time of life."

Jean was a little troubled, and did not like to see me treat the matter so lightly; but I said it was best to treat it so, for there was nothing serious about it. This morning I sent the sorrowful facts of this day's irremediable disaster to the Associated Press. Will both appear in this evening's papers?—the one so blithe, the other so tragic?

I lost Susy thirteen years ago; I lost her mother— her incomparable mother!—five and a half years ago; Clara has gone away to live in Europe; and now I have lost Jean. How poor I am, who was once so rich! Seven months ago Mr. Roger died—one of the best friends I ever had, and the nearest perfect, as man and gentleman, I have yet met among my race; within the last six weeks Gilder has passed away, and Laffan—old, old friends of mine. Jean lies yonder, I sit here; we are strangers under our own roof; we kissed hands good-by at this door last night—

and it was forever, we never suspecting it. She lies there, and I sit here—writing, busying myself, to keep my heart from breaking. How dazzlingly the sunshine is flooding the hills around! It is like a mockery.

Seventy-four years old, twenty-four days ago. Seventy-four years old yesterday. Who can estimate my age today?

I have looked upon her again. I wonder I can bear it. She looks just as her mother looked when she lay dead in that Florentine villa so long ago. The sweet placidity of death! it is more beautiful than sleep.

I saw her mother buried. I said I would never endure that horror again; that I would never again look into the grave of any one dear to me. I have kept to that. They will take Jean from this house tomorrow, and bear her to Elmira,

New York, where lie those of us that have been released, but I shall not follow.

Jean was on the dock when the ship came in, only four days ago. She was at the door, beaming a welcome, when I reached this house the next evening. We played cards, and she tried to teach me a new game called "Mark Twain." We sat chatting cheerily in the library last night, and she wouldn't let me look into the loggia, where she was making Christmas preparations. She said she would finish them in the morning, and then her little French friend would arrive from New York—the surprise would follow; the surprise she had been working over for days. While she was out for a moment I disloyally stole a look. The loggia floor was clothed with rugs and furnished with chairs and sofas; and the uncompleted surprise was there: in the form of a Christmas tree that was drenched with silver film in a most wonderful way; and on a table was prodigal profusion of bright things which she was going to hang upon it today. What desecrating hand will ever banish that eloquent unfinished surprise from that place? Not mine, surely. All these little matters have happened in the last four days. "Little." Yes—*then*. But not now. Nothing she said or thought or did is little now. And all the lavish humor!—what is become of it? It is pathos, now. Pathos, and the thought of it brings tears.

All these little things happened such a few hours ago—and now she lies yonder. Lies yonder, and cares for nothing any more. Strange—marvelous—incredible! I have had this experience before; but it would still be incredible if I had had it a thousand times.

"Miss Jean is dead!"

That is what Katy said. When I heard the door open behind the bed's head without a preliminary knock, I supposed it was Jean coming to kiss me good morning, she being the only person who was used to entering without formalities.

And so—

I have been to Jean's parlor. Such a turmoil of Christmas presents for servants and friends! They are everywhere; tables, chairs, sofas, the floor—everything is occupied, and over-occupied. It is many and many a year since I have seen the like. In that ancient day Mrs. Clemens and I used to slip softly into the nursery at midnight on Christmas Eve and look the array of presents over. The children were little then. And now here is Jean's parlor looking just as that nursery used to look. The presents are not labeled—the hands are forever idle that would have labeled them today. Jean's mother always worked herself down with her Christmas preparations. Jean did the same yesterday and the preceding days, and the fatigue has cost her her life. The fatigue caused the convulsion that attacked her this morning. She had had no attack for months.

Jean was so full of life and energy that she was constantly is danger of overtaxing her strength. Every morning she was in the saddle by half past seven, and off to the station for her mail. She examined the letters and I distributed them: some to her, some to Mr. Paine, the others to the stenographer and myself. She dispatched her share and then mounted her horse again and went around superintending her farm and her poultry the rest of the day. Sometimes she played billiards with me after dinner, but she was usually too tired to play, and went early to bed.

Yesterday afternoon I told her about some plans I had been devising while absent in Bermuda, to lighten her burdens. We would get a housekeeper; also we would put her share of the secretary-work into Mr. Paine's hands.

No—she wasn't willing. She had been making plans herself. The matter ended in a compromise, I submitted. I always did. She wouldn't audit the bills and let Paine fill out the checks—she would continue to attend to that herself. Also, she would continue to be housekeeper, and let Katy assist. Also, she would continue to answer the letters of personal friends for me. Such was the compromise. Both of us called it by that name, though I was not able to see where my formidable change had been made.

However, Jean was pleased, and that was sufficient for me. She was proud of being my secretary, and I was never able to persuade her to give up any part of her share in that unlovely work.

In the talk last night I said I found everything going so smoothly that if she were willing I would go back to Bermuda in February and get blessedly out of the clash and turmoil again for another month. She was urgent that I should do it, and said that if I would put off the trip until March she would take Katy and go with me. We struck hands upon that, and said it was settled. I had a mind to write to Bermuda by tomorrow's ship and secure a furnished house and servants. I meant to write the letter this morning. But it will never be written, now.

For she lies yonder, and before her is another journey than that.

Night is closing down; the rim of the sun barely shows above the skyline of the hills.

I have been looking at that face again that was growing dearer and dearer to me every day. I was getting acquainted with Jean in these last nine months. She had been long an exile from home when she came to us three-quarters of a year ago. She had been shut up in sanitariums, many miles from us. How eloquent glad and grateful she was to cross her father's threshold again!

Would I bring her back to life if I could do it? I would not. If a word would do it, I would beg for strength to withhold the word. And I would have the strength; I am sure of it. In her loss I am almost bankrupt, and my life is a bitterness, but I am content: for she has been enriched with the most precious of all gifts—that gift which makes all other gifts mean and poor—death. I have never wanted any released friend of mine restored to life since I reached manhood. I felt in this way when Susy passed away; and later my wife, and later Mr. Rogers. When Clara met me at the station in New York and told me Mr. Rogers had died suddenly that morning, my thought was, Oh, favorite of fortune—fortunate all his long and lovely life—fortunate to his latest moment! The reporters said there were tears of sorrow in my eyes. True—but they were for *me*, not for him. He had suffered no loss. All the fortunes he had ever made before were poverty compared with this one.

Why did I build this house, two years ago? To shelter this vast emptiness? How foolish I was! But I shall stay in it. The spirits of the dead hallow a house, for me. It was not so with other members of the family. Susy died in the house we built in Hartford. Mrs. Clemens would never enter it again. But it made the house dearer to me. I have entered it once since, when it was tenantless and silent and forlorn, but to me it was a holy place and beautiful. It seemed to me that the spirits of the dead were all about me, and would speak to me and welcome me if they could: Livy, and Susy, and George, and Henry Robinson, and Charles Dudley Warner. How good and kind they were, and how lovable their lives! In fancy I could see them all again, I could call the children back and hear them romp again with George—that peerless black ex-slave and children's idol who came one day—a flitting stranger—to wash windows, and stayed eighteen years. Until he died. Clara and Jean would never enter again the New York hotel which their mother had frequented in earlier days. They could not bear it. But I shall stay in this house. It is dearer to me tonight than ever it was before. Jean's spirit will make it beautiful for me always. Her lonely and tragic death—but I will not think of that now.

Jean's mother always devoted two or three weeks to Christmas shopping, and was always physically exhausted when Christmas Eve came. Jean was her very own child—she wore herself out present-hunting in New York these latter days. Paine has just found on her desk a long list of names—fifty, he thinks—people to whom she sent presents last night. Apparently she forgot no one. And Katy found there a roll of bank-notes, for the servants.

Her dog has been wandering about the grounds today, comradeless and forlorn. I have seen him from the windows. She got him from Germany. He has tall ears and looks exactly like a wolf. He was educated in Germany, and knows no language but the German. Jean gave him no orders save in that tongue. And so when the burglar-alarm made a fierce clamor at midnight a fortnight ago, the butler, who is French and knows no German, tried in vain to interest the dog in the supposed burglar. Jean wrote me, to Bermuda, about the incident. It was the last letter I was ever to receive from her bright head and her competent hand. The dog will not be neglected.

There was never a kinder heart than Jean's. From her childhood up she always spent the most of her allowance on charities of one kind or another. After she became secretary and had her income doubled she spent her money upon these things with a free hand. Mine too, I am glad and grateful to say.

She was a loyal friend to all animals, and she loved them all, birds, beasts, and everything—even snakes—an inheritance from me. She knew all the birds; she was high up in that lore. She became a member of various humane societies when she was still a little girl—both here and abroad—and she remained an active member to the last. She founded two or three societies for the protection of animals, here and in Europe.

She was an embarrassing secretary, for she fished my correspondence out of the waste-basket and answered the letters. She thought all letters deserved the courtesy of an answer. Her mother brought her up in that kindly error.

She could write a good letter, and was swift with her pen. She had but an indifferent ear for music, but her tongue took to languages with an easy facility. She never allowed her Italian, French, and German to get rusty through neglect.

The telegrams of sympathy are flowing in, from far and wide, now, just as they did in Italy five years and a half ago, when this child's mother laid down her blameless life. They cannot heal the hurt, but they take away some of the pain. When Jean and I kissed hands and parted at my door last, how little did we imagine that in twenty-two hours the telegraph would be bringing words like these:

"From the bottom of our hearts we send out sympathy, dearest of friends."

For many and many a day to come, wherever I go in this house, remembrancers of Jean will mutely speak to me of her. Who can count the number of them?

She was in exile two years with the hope of healing her malady—epilepsy. There are no words to express how grateful I am that she did not meet her fate in the hands of strangers, but in the loving shelter of her own home.

"Miss Jean is dead!"

It is true. Jean is dead.

A month ago I was writing bubbling and hilarious articles for magazines yet to appear, and now I am writing—this.

Christmas Day. Noon.—Last night I went to Jean's room at intervals, and turned back the sheet and looked at the peaceful face, and kissed the cold brow, and remembered that heartbreaking night in Florence so long ago, in that cavernous and silent vast villa, when I crept downstairs so many times, and turned back a sheet and looked at a face just like this one—Jean's mother's face—and kissed a brow that was just like this one.

And last night I saw again what I had seen then—that strange and lovely Miracle—the sweet, soft contours of early maidenhood restored by the gracious hand of death! When Jean's mother lay dead, all trace of care, and trouble, and suffering, and the corroding years had vanished out of the face, and I was looking again upon it as I had known and worshipped it in its young bloom and beauty a whole generation before.

About three in the morning, while wandering about the house in the deep silences, as one does in times like these, when there is a dumb sense that something has been lost that will never be found again, yet must be sought, if only for the employment the useless seeking gives, I came upon Jean's dog in the hall downstairs, and noted that he did not spring to greet me, according to his hospitable habit, but came slow and sorrowfully; also I remembered that he had not visited Jean's apartment since the tragedy. Poor fellow, did he know? I think so. Always when Jean was abroad in the open he was with her; always when she was in the house he was with her, in the night as well as in the day. Her parlor was his bedroom. Whenever I happened upon him on the ground floor he always followed me about, and when I went upstairs he went too—in a tumultuous gallop. But now it was different: after patting him a little I went to the library—he remained behind; when I went upstairs he did not follow me, save with his wistful eyes. He has wonderful eyes—big, and kind, and eloquent. He can talk with them. He is a beautiful creature, and is of the breed of the New York police-dogs. I do not like dogs, because they bark when there is no occasion for it; but I have liked this one from the beginning, because he belonged to Jean, and because he never barks except when there is occasion—which is not oftener than twice a week.

In my wanderings I visited Jean's parlor. On a shelf I found a pile of my books, and I knew what it meant. She was waiting for me to come home from Bermuda and autograph them, then she would send them away. If I only knew whom she intended them for! But I shall never know. I will keep them. Her hand has touched them—it is an accolade—they are noble, now.

And in a closet she had hidden a surprise for me—a thing I have often wished I owned: a noble big globe. I couldn't see it for the tears. She will never know the pride I take in it, and the pleasure. Today the mails are full of loving remembrances for her: full of those old, old kind words she loved so well, "Merry Christmas to Jean!" If she could only have lived one day longer!

At last she ran out of money, and would not use mine. So she sent to one of those New York homes for poor girls all the clothes she could spare—and more, most likely.

Christmas Night.—This afternoon they took her away from her room. As soon as I might, I went down to the library, and there she lay, in her coffin, dressed in exactly the same clothes she wore when she stood at the other end of the same room on the 6th of October last, as Clara's chief bridesmaid. Her face was radiant with happy excitement then; it was the same face now, with the dignity of death and the peace of God upon it.

They told me the first mourner to come was the dog. He came uninvited, and stood up on his hind legs and rested his fore paws upon the trestle, and took a last long look at the face that was so dear to him, then went his way as silently as he had come. *He knows.*

At mid-afternoon it began to snow. The pity of it—that Jean could not see it! She so loved the snow.

The snow continued to fall. At six o'clock the hearse drew up to the door to bear away its pathetic burden. As they lifted the casket, Paine began playing on the orchestrelle Schubert's "Impromptu," which was Jean's favorite. Then he played the Intermezzo; that was for Susy; then he played the Largo; that was for their mother. He did this at my request. Elsewhere in my Autobiography I have told how the Intermezzo and the Largo came to be associated in my heart with Susy and Livy in their last hours in this life.

From my windows I saw the hearse and the carriages wind along the road and gradually grow vague and spectral in the falling snow, and presently disappear. Jean was gone out of my life, and would not come back any more. Jervis, the cousin she had played with when they were babies together—he and her beloved old Katy—were conducting her to her distant childhood home, where she will lie by her mother's side once more, in the company of Susy and Langdon.

December 26th. The dog came to see me at eight o'clock this morning. He was very affectionate, poor orphan! My room will be his quarters hereafter.

The storm raged all night. It has raged all the morning. The snow drives across the landscape in vast clouds, superb, sublime—and Jean not here to see.

2:30 P.M.—It is the time appointed. The funeral has begun. Four hundred miles away, but I can see it all, just as if I were there. The scene is the library in the Langdon homestead. Jean's coffin stands where her mother and I stood, forty years ago, and were married; and where Susy's coffin stood thirteen years ago; where her mother's stood five years and a half ago; and where mine will stand after a little time.

Five o'clock.—It is all over.

When Clara went away two weeks ago to live in Europe, it was hard, but I could bear it, for I had Jean left. I said *we* would be a family. We said we would be close comrades and happy—just we two. That fair dream was in my mind when Jean met me at the steamer last Monday; it was in my mind when she received me at the door last Tuesday evening. We were together; *we were a family!* the dream had come true—oh, precisely true, contentedly, true, satisfyingly true! and remained true two whole days.

And now? Now Jean is in her grave!

In the grave—if I can believe it. God rest her sweet spirit!

Appendix D
Major Mark Twain Web Sites

The Mark Twain House, Hartford, Connecticut:
http://www.marktwainhouse.org/

The Center for Mark Twain Studies, Elmira College, New York:
http://www.elmira.edu/academics/ar_marktwain.shtml

Mark Twain Sites in Elmira, New York:
http://lemur.cit.cornell.edu/~jules/Mark_Twain.html

The Mark Twain Papers and Project, the Bancroft Library, the University of California, Berkeley:
http://bancroft.berkeley.edu/MTP/

TwainWeb, The Mark Twain Forum (reviews, archive material):
http://www.yorku.ca/twainweb/

Mark Twain scholar Jim Zwick's page (excellent resource):
http://www.boondocksnet.com/twainwww/

Mark Twain Circular (The Mark Twain Circle of America):
http://www.citadel.edu/faculty/leonard/mtcircular.htm

Mark Twain Official Homepage
http://www.cmgww.com/historic/twain/

Home page for Hannibal, Missouri, Twain's boyhood home:
http://www.hanmo.com/

Hannibal.net (Site about Mark Twain's life and works):
http://www.hannibal.net/twain/

The Mark Twain Circle of New York (Peter Salwen's site):
http://salwen.com/mtahome.html

Mark Twain in His Times Homepage (by Stephen Railton, Department of English, University of Virginia):
http://etext.virginia.edu/railton/

American Writers: Mark Twain (C-SPAN site):
http://www.americanwriters.org/writers/twain.asp

Mark Twain: A Film Directed by Ken Burns (PBS site):
http://www.pbs.org/marktwain/

Mark Twain Quotations, Newspaper Collections, & Related Resources (Twain researcher Barbara Schmidt's site):
http://www.twainquotes.com/

PAL: Perspectives in American Literature—A Research and Reference Guide (by Paul P. Reuben)
http://www.csustan.edu/english/reuben/pal/chap5/twain.html

Notes and Sources

1 *There is a drama, a comedy, and a tragedy* Mark Twain, "The Refuge of the Derelicts," printed in *Mark Twain's Fables of Man*, ed. John S. Tuckey (Berkeley, University of California Press, 1972), p. 197.

2 *This was the image fiercely protected* Hamlin Hill, *Mark Twain: God's Fool* (New York: Harper and Row, 1973) The author summarizes the guarding of Mark Twain's image in his introduction, pp. xv–xvi.

3 *profound personal tragedy* CBS press release issued April 13, 1960.

4 *Mark Twain was immensely interested* Hamlin Hill, *Mark Twain: God's Fool*, p. xvii.

5 *They didn't want to hear it* Horton Foote, taped interview with the author, September 2000.

6 *I don't even know if a copy exists* Horton Foote, taped interview with the author, December 1997.

7 *My true influences as a vastly obsessive* Horton Foote, taped interview with the author, September 2000.

8 *I was very fond of* Horton Foote, taped interview with the author, September 2000.

9 *propel a television writer* David Bianculli, *Dictionary of Teleliteracy* (New York: Continuum, 1996), p. 189.

10 *ability to nurture writers* David Bianculli, *Dictionary of Teleliteracy* (New York: Continuum, 1996), p. 246.

11 *I remember the genesis of this* Horton Foote, taped interview with the author, September 2000.

12 *the pinnacle of live drama* Tim Brooks and Earle Marsh, *The Complete Directory to Prime Time Network and Cable TV Shows:*

1946–Present (New York: Ballantine Books, seventh edition, 1999), p. 811.

13 *Remember the play you wrote* Fred Coe quote recalled by Horton Foote during taped interview with the author, September 2000.

14 *part steamboat, part medieval stronghold* Justin Kaplan, *Mr. Clemens and Mark Twain* (New York: Simon & Schuster, 1966), p. 181.

15 *deliberate revenge for the poverty* Hamlin Hill, *Mark Twain: God's Fool* (New York: Harper and Row, 1973), p. 5.

16 *our house was not* Mark Twain quoted in Albert Bigelow Paine's three-volume *Mark Twain: A Biography* (New York: Harper and Brothers, 1912), pp. 1023–24.

17 *live in literature* Mark Twain, January 1894 letter to his wife, *Mark Twain's Letters* (New York: Harper and Brothers Publishers, 1917), p. 607.

18 *In the thick of the fight* Mark Twain, April 1894 letter to his wife, *Mark Twain's Letters* (New York: Harper and Brothers Publishers, 1917), p. 614.

19 *Do you remember, Livy* Clara Clemens, *My Father: Mark Twain* (New York: Harper and Brothers Publishers, 1931), p. 179.

20 *the only man who is* Mark Twain, February 1894 letter to his wife, *Mark Twain's Letters* (New York: Harper and Brothers Publishers, 1917), pp. 612–13.

21 *dreamed of being rich* Justin Kaplan, *Mark Twain and His World* (New York: Simon and Schuster, 1974), p. 190.

22 *We are a very happy family* Mark Twain, *The Autobiography of Mark Twain*, edited by Charles Neider (New York: Harper and Brothers, Publishers, 1959), p. 203.

23 *It is one of the mysteries* Mark Twain, *The Autobiography of Mark Twain*, edited by Charles Neider (New York: Harper and Brothers, Publishers, 1959), p. 323.

24 *All my life I have* Mark Twain, 1895 letter to Henry H. Rogers, *Mark Twain's Letters* (New York: Harper and Brothers Publishers, 1917), pp. 621–22.

25 *The research was intense* Horton Foote, taped interview with the author, September 2000.

26 *for Mark Twain's daughter* Mark Twain, *Mark Twain's Notebook* (New York: Harper and Brothers, 1935), p. 319.

27 *Humor is the great thing* Mark Twain, "What Paul Bourget Thinks of Us," 1895 essay.

28 *hunting for a crime* Justin Kaplan, *Mark Twain and His World* (New York: Simon and Schuster, 1974), p. 160.

29 *If man is not* Bernard DeVoto, *Mark Twain at Work* (Boston: Houghton Mifflin Company, 1967 reprint of 1942 book), p. 116.

30 *It was a pleasure* Sandy Kenyon, taped interview with the author, February 2002.

31 *He was really wonderful* Horton Foote, taped interview with the author, September 2000.

32 *But that was a period* Hal Holbrook, taped interview with the author, April 2001.

33 *We hadn't thought of him* Horton Foote, taped interview with the author, September 2000.

34 *His private life was* Horton Foote, taped interview with the author, September 2000.

35 *out of the corner of* Marc Scott Zicree *The Twilight Zone Companion* (New York: Bantam Books, 1982), p. 202.

36 *I did four shows with* John Frankenheimer, taped interview with the author, January 2002.

37 *It was the first time* Horton Foote, taped interview with the author, September 2000.

38 *It takes three hours* Franchot Tone, quoted by Mary Lee Morken, "Actor Long Acquainted with Twain," *The Elmira Advertiser,* October 14, 1960.

39 *We did it all in one* Shirley Knight, taped interview with the author, September 2000.

40 *He seemed more like* Ida Langdon, quoted in "Festival Commemorates 3 Anniversaries of Mark Twain," *The Octagon,* (Elmira College newspaper), October 6, 1960, p. 1.

41 *If Miss Langdon liked it best* Franchot Tone, quoted by Peggy Gallagher, "Franchot To Give Twain Tone," *The Elmira Star-Gazette,* October 14, 1960, p. 1.

42 *My association with Mark Twain* Franchot Tone, quoted by Mary Lee Morken, "Actor Long Acquainted with Twain," *The Elmira Advertiser,* October 14, 1960.

43 *was a ham at heart* Franchot Tone, quoted in "Franchot Tone Draws 500 For Mark Twain Portrayal," *The Elmira Advertiser*, October 15, 1960.

44 *Franchot Tone was an absolute joy* Shirley Knight, taped interview with the author, September 2000.

45 *It really was a wonderful era* Shirley Knight, taped interview with the author, September 2000.

46 *My husband tried writing for* Shirley Knight, taped interview with the author, September 2000.

47 *Horton was very intent* Shirley Knight, taped interview with the author, September 2000.

Bibliography

Andrews, Kenneth R. *Nook Farm: Mark Twain's Hartford Circle.* Cambridge: Harvard University Press, 1950.

Baetzhold, Howard G. *Mark Twain & John Bull: The British Connection.* Bloomington: Indiana University Press, 1970.

Barnouw, Erik. *Tube of Plenty* (second edition) New York: Oxford University Press, 1990.

Bianculli, David. *Dictionary of Teleliteracy.* New York: Continuum, 1996.

Branch, Edgar. *The Literary Apprenticeship of Mark Twain.* Urbana: University of Illinois Press, 1950.

Brooks, Tim and Earle Marsh, *The Complete Directory to Prime Time Network and Cable TV Shows: 1946–Present (seventh edition).* New York: Ballantine Books, 1999.

Brown, Les. *Les Brown's Encyclopedia of Television* (third edition). Detroit: Visible Ink Press, 1992.

Budd, Louis J. *Mark Twain: Social Philosopher.* Bloomington: Indiana University Press, 1962.

Burlingame, Jon. *TV's Biggest Hits: The Story of Television Themes from "Dragnet" to "Friends."* New York: Schirmer Books, 1996.

Campbell, Robert. *The Golden Years of Broadcasting: A Celebration of the First 50 Years of Radio and TV On NBC.* New York: Charles Scribner's Sons, 1976.

Castleman, Harry, and Walter J. Podrazik. *Watching TV: Four Decades of American Television.* New York: McGraw-Hill Book Company, 1982.

Clemens, Clara. *My Father: Mark Twain.* New York: Harper and Brothers, 1911.

Clemens, Susy. *Papa: An Intimate Biography of Mark Twain* (edited by Charles Neider). New York: Doubleday, 1985.

Connors, Martin, and Jim Craddock, eds. *VideoHound's Golden Movie Retriever.* Detroit: Visible Ink Press, 1999.

DeVoto, Bernard. *Mark Twain at Work.* Cambridge: Harvard University Press, 1942.

DeVoto, Bernard. *Mark Twain's America.* Boston: Little, Brown and Company, 1932.

Eble, Kenneth E. *Old Clemens and W.D.H.: The Story of a Remarkable Friendship.* Baton Rouge: Louisiana State University Press, 1985.

Engel, Joel. *Rod Serling: The Dreams and Nightmares of Life in the Twilight Zone.* Chicago: Contemporary Books, 1989.

Fatout, Paul. *Mark Twain on the Lecture Circuit.* Bloomington: University of Indiana Press, 1960.

Ferguson, DeLancey, *Mark Twain: Man and Legend.* New York: Bobbs-Merrill, 1943.

Fireman, Judy, ed. *TV Book: The Ultimate Television Book.* New York: Workman Publishing Company, 1977.

Fishkin, Shelley Fisher. *Lighting Out for the Territory: Reflections on Mark Twain and American Culture.* New York: Oxford University Press, 1997.

Fishkin, Shelley Fisher. *Was Huck Black? Mark Twain and African-American Voices.* New York: Oxford University Press, 1993.

Foote, Horton. *Farewell: A Memoir of a Texas Childhood.* New York: Scribner, 1999.

Foote, Horton. *Three Plays (Old Man, Tomorrow, Roots in a Parched Ground).* New York: Harcourt, Brace, 1962.

Foote, Horton. *Three Screenplays (To Kill a Mockingbird, Tender Mercies, and The Trip to Bountiful).* New York: Grove Press, 1989.

Foote, Horton. *The Young Man from Atlanta.* New York: Dutton, 1995.

Geismar, Maxwell. *Mark Twain: American Prophet.* Boston: Houghton Mifflin, 1970.

Gibson, William M. *The Art of Mark Twain.* New York: Oxford University Press, 1976.

Goldstein, Fred, and Stan Goldstein. *Prime-Time Television: A Pictorial History from Milton Berle to "Falcon Crest."* New York: Crown Publishers, Inc., 1983.

Harnsberger, Caroline Thomas. *Mark Twain: Family Man.* New York: The Citadel Press, 1960.

Heldenfels, R.D. *Television's Greatest Year: 1954.* New York: Continuum, 1994.

Hill, Hamlin. *Mark Twain: God's Fool.* New York: Harper and Row, 1973.

Holbrook, Hal. *Mark Twain Tonight!* New York: Ives Washburn, 1959.

Howells, William Dean. *My Mark Twain.* New York: Harper and Brothers, 1910.

Kaplan, Justin. *Mark Twain and His World.* New York: Simon and Schuster, 1974.

Kaplan, Justin. *Mr. Clemens and Mark Twain.* New York: Simon and Schuster, 1966.

Katz, Ephraim. *The Film Encyclopedia* (third edition revised by Fred Klein and Ronald Dean Nolen). New York: HarperPerennial, 1998.

Lawton, Mary. *A Lifetime With Mark Twain: The Memories of Katy Leary.* New York: Harcourt, Brace, 1925.

LeMaster, J.R., and James D. Wilson, eds. *The Mark Twain Encyclopedia.* New York: Garland, 1993.

Lorch, Fred W. *The Trouble Begins at Eight: Mark Twain's Lecture Tours.* Ames: Iowa State University, 1968.

Maltin, Leonard, ed. *Leonard Maltin's Movie & Video Guide: 1999 Edition.* New York: Plume, 1998.

Martin, Mick and Marsha Porter. *Video Movie Guide 1999.* New York: Ballantine Books, 1998.

McCarty, John, and Brian Kelleher. *Alfred Hitchcock Presents: An Illustrated Guide to the Ten-Year Television Career of the Master of Suspense.* New York: St. Martin's Press, 1985.

McNeil, Alex, *Total Television: A Comprehensive Guide to Programming from 1948 to the Present* (third edition). New York: Penguin Books, 1991.

Meltzer, Milton. *Mark Twain Himself.* New York: Thomas Y. Crowell, 1960.

Monaco, James (and the editors of Baseline). *The Movie Guide: A Comprehensive, Alphabetical Listing of the Most Important Movies Ever Made.* New York: Perigee, 1992.

Monush, Barry (ed.) *International Television & Video Almanac.* New York: Quigley Publishing Company, 1992.

O'Neil, Thomas. *The Emmys: The Ultimate Unofficial Guide to the Battle of TV's Best Shows and Greatest Stars* (third edition). New York: Perigee, 2000.

Paine, Albert Bigelow. *Mark Twain, A Biography: The Personal and Literary Life of Samuel Langhorne Clemens* (three volumes). New York: Harper and Brothers, 1912.

Parish, James Robert, and Vincent Terrace. *The Complete Actors' Television Credits, 1948–88* (second edition). Metuchen, New Jersey: The Scarecrow Press, Inc., 1989.

Quick, Dorothy. *Enchantment: A Little Girl's Friendship With Mark Twain.* Norman: University of Oklahoma Press, 1961.

Rasmussen, R. Kent. *Mark Twain A to Z: The Essential Reference to His Life and Writings.* New York: Facts On File, 1995.

Rasmussen, R. Kent, ed. *The Quotable Mark Twain: His Essential Aphorisms, Witticisms & Concise Opinions.* Chicago: Contemporary Books, 1997.

Robinson, Marc. *Brought to You in Living Color: 75 Years of Great Moments in Television & Radio from NBC.* New York: John Wiley & Sons, Inc., 2002.

Salsbury, Edith Colgate, ed. *Susy and Mark Twain.* New York: Harper and Row, 1965.

Sander, Gordon F. *Serling: The Rise and Twilight of Television's Last Angry Man.* New York: Dutton, 1992.

Schow, David J., and Jeffrey Frentzen. *The Outer Limits: The Official Companion.* New York: Ace Science Fiction Books, 1986.

Serling, Rod. *Patterns: Four Television Plays.* New York: Bantam Books, 1958.

Skelton, Scott, and Jim Benson. *Rod Serling's Night Gallery: An After-Hours Tour.* Syracuse: Syracuse University Press, 1999.

Tenney, Thomas A. *Mark Twain: A Reference Guide.* Boston: G.K. Hall, 1977.

Terrace, Vincent. *Encyclopedia of Television: Series, Pilots and Specials, 1937–73.* New York: Zoetrope, 1986.

Terrace, Vincent. *Encyclopedia of Television: Series, Pilots and Specials, 1974–84.* New York: Zoetrope, 1986.

Twain, Mark (Samuel Clemens). *The Autobiography of Mark Twain* (edited by Charles Neider). New York: Harper and Brothers, 1959.

Twain, Mark (Samuel Clemens). *A Connecticut Yankee in King Arthur's Court.* New York: Charles L. Webster, 1889.

Twain, Mark (Samuel Clemens). *Following the Equator.* Hartford: American Publishing Company, 1897.

Twain, Mark (Samuel Clemens). *Life On the Mississippi.* Boston: James R. Osgood, 1883.

Twain, Mark. *The Love Letters of Mark Twain* (edited by Dixon Wecter). New York: Harper and Brothers, 1949.

Twain, Mark, and William Dean Howells. *Mark Twain-Howells Letters: The Correspondence of Samuel L. Clemens and William Dean Howells, 1872–1910* (two volumes edited by Henry Nash Smith and William M. Gibson). Cambridge: Harvard University Press, 1960.

Twain, Mark (Samuel Clemens). *Mark Twain in Eruption* (edited by Bernard DeVoto). New York: Harper and Brothers, 1940.

Twain, Mark (Samuel Clemens). *Mark Twain's Autobiography* (two volumes, edited by Albert Bigelow Paine). New York: Harper and Brothers, 1924.

Twain, Mark (Samuel Clemens). *Mark Twain's Fables of Man* (edited by John S. Tuckey). Berkeley: University of California Press, 1972.

Twain, Mark (Samuel Clemens). *Mark Twain's Letters* (two volumes, edited by Albert Bigelow Paine). New York: Harper and Brothers Publishers, 1917.

Twain, Mark (Samuel Clemens). *Mark Twain's Notebook* (edited by Albert Bigelow Paine). New York: Harper and Brothers, 1935.

Twain, Mark (Samuel Clemens). *What Is Man?* New York: De Vinne Press, 1906.

Twain, Mark (Samuel Clemens). *What Is Man? and Other Essays* (edited by Albert Bigelow Paine). New York: Harper and Brothers, 1917.

Wagenknecht, Edward. *Mark Twain: The Man and His Work.* New Haven: Yale University Press, 1945.

Ward, Geoffrey C., Dayton Duncan, and Ken Burns. *Mark Twain: An Illustrated Biography.* New York: Alfred A. Knopf, 2001.

Webster, Samuel Charles, ed. *Mark Twain: Business Man.* Boston: Little, Brown, and Company, 1946.

Wiley, Mason, and Damien Bona. *Inside Oscar: The Unofficial History of the Academy Awards* (tenth edition). New York: Ballantine Books, 1996.

Willis, Resa. *Mark and Livy: The Love Story of Mark Twain and the Woman Who Almost Tamed Him.* New York: Atheneum Publishers, 1992.

Zicreee, Marc Scott. *The Twilight Zone Companion.* New York: Bantam Books, 1982.

Zinman, David. *50 Classic Motion Pictures: The Stuff that Dreams Are Made of.* New York: Bonanza Books, 1970.

HORTON FOOTE is one of America's leading playwrights. His works include the 1995 Pulitzer Prize winner, *The Young Man From Atlanta*, and the Academy Award–winning screenplay for *To Kill a Mocking Bird*. He won an Emmy for the 1997 Hallmark Hall of Fame version of *Old Man*, and was a recipient of the National Medal of Arts Award in 2000. PHOTO © MARION ETTLINGER

MARK DAWIDZIAK is the television critic at the *Cleveland Plain Dealer*. A theatre, film, and TV reviewer for more than twenty years, his six previous books include *The Barter Theatre Story: Love Made Visible, The Columbo Phile, Mark My Words: Mark Twain on Writing*, and *The Night Stalker Companion*. He has also authored three plays, including *The Reports of My Death Are Greatly Exaggerated*, a two-act adaptation of several Mark Twain sketches. He lives in Cuyahoga Falls, Ohio. PHOTO © PAUL BAUER